PowerPoint 365 for Beginners

POWERPOINT 365 ESSENTIALS - BOOK 1

M.L. HUMPHREY

SELECT TITLES BY M.L. HUMPHREY

EXCEL 365 ESSENTIALS
Excel 365 for Beginners
Intermediate Excel 365

102 Useful Excel 365 Functions

WORD 365 ESSENTIALS
Word 365 for Beginners
Intermediate Word 365

POWERPOINT 365 ESSENTIALS
PowerPoint 365 for Beginners
Intermediate PowerPoint 365

See mlhumphrey.com for more titles

CONTENTS

CONTENTS (CONT.)

Introduction

PowerPoint is a great tool if you need to present information. And it's an essential tool to learn in a number of corporate environments. I'm almost twenty-five years into my corporate career and I've yet to work for an employer who didn't use PowerPoint. These days there are sometimes other, similar options available, but PowerPoint is still that gold-standard program.

And the nice thing about mastering PowerPoint is that most of the other programs out there are based upon the same principles and concepts, so master one, you're pretty close to understanding the others.

But before we get started, we need to discuss what this particular book covers and one little issue you need to keep in mind. This book is written using PowerPoint 365 as it existed in October 2023.

All Microsoft 365 programs are a bit of a moving target because they continuously update, so your version of 365 may differ slightly.

The basics tend to stay the same so it shouldn't prevent you from learning how to use PowerPoint, but there will be changes over time.

For example, I have a different recommendation in this book about using presentation themes than I did in the original *PowerPoint for Beginners* or in *PowerPoint 2019 Beginner*. The October 2023 version of PowerPoint 365 has changed just enough to warrant that.

So I can't guarantee for you that they won't shift things again in the future. That's the risk you take using 365.

Still, the basics tend to be the basics. And the more beginner-level a book the more stable things should be. Just know that with 365 it's not set in stone the way that versions like PowerPoint 2019 are.

Another thing to be aware of is the issue of backwards compatibility. That's the ability to work with those who have an older version of the same program. If you use a tool that was just released, chances are anyone with an older version of that same program won't have the same experience you do. So when you work with a wide range of users, it is best to stick to core functions and keep it simple.

This is probably most important when collaborating with someone on creating a presentation, but it may also come up if you travel around a lot and have to present in a wide variety of settings. If you're using their computer, they may not have the same version of PowerPoint you do.

Limit yourself to the basic functionality of PowerPoint and you should be pretty safe, but it's something to be aware of. And if backwards compatibility is something you really need to keep in mind, then you may be better off learning from *PowerPoint for Beginners* or *PowerPoint 2019 Beginner*, which were written using older versions of PowerPoint. Or maybe even saving your files as .ppt files instead of .pptx files, although that may be more than you need to do.

Just keep it in mind. You should be fine, but I mention it so you're aware that it's a potential issue.

Finally, I'm going to assume here that you have worked in Word or Excel and know the basics of formatting text, etc. I will cover those topics again here just not at the same granular level of detail. If you're brand new to all Office programs, I'd recommend starting with Word first.

Okay then, let's get started by talking about how to change the appearance of PowerPoint.

PowerPoint Appearance

All of the screenshots in this book are going to be made using the Colorful theme in PowerPoint. It will look like this on the main screen when you're looking at a blank presentation:

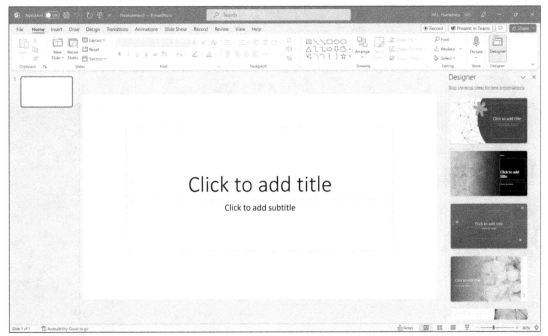

Note the orange color at the top. Also note that the background is light gray and the tasks have a white or lighter gray background behind them.

This is the Dark Gray theme:

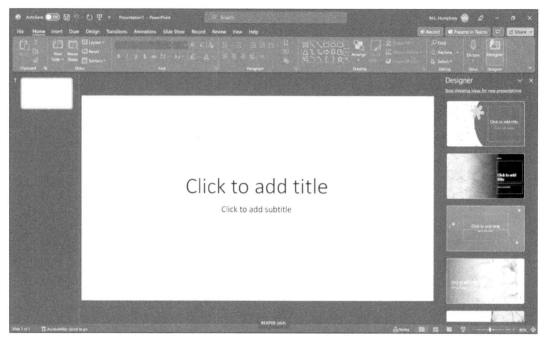

Note that the top and areas around the slide are now dark gray and the main section of options is a lighter dark gray. And that the text in those sections is white.

Another option is the Black theme which looks like this:

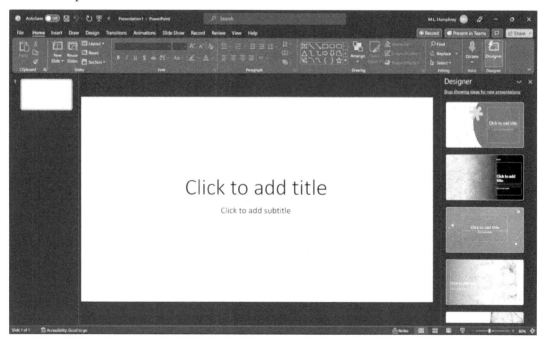

With this one, the top and surrounding areas are black and the options area is a darker gray or lighter black and the text is white.

Finally, there is a White option which looks like this:

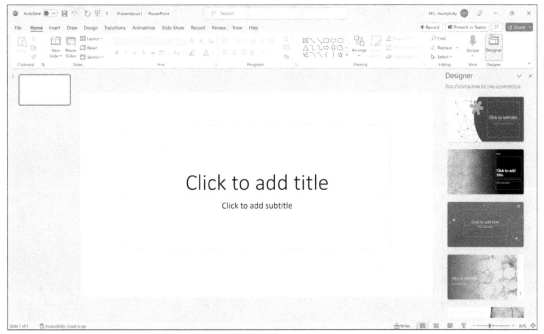

It's much the same as the Colorful option but doesn't have the orange strip across the top.

Those are the options available within PowerPoint itself, but your system settings can also impact the appearance of PowerPoint, too.

If you want your version of PowerPoint to match my screenshots, use either the White or Colorful themes, and the default system settings for Windows.

If you work with other settings, it may mean that at times I tell you something is one color when it's actually a different color for you. Do what makes you most comfortable, just keep that difference in mind.

Your office theme in PowerPoint can be changed from the Welcome screen. This should appear by default when you open PowerPoint, but if it doesn't it can also be found by clicking on the File tab from an open presentation. (Don't worry if you don't know how to do either of those, we will cover both in the Absolute Basics chapter and you can then come back here if you want to change your settings.)

The first way to change your Office Theme is to go to the Options setting at the bottom left corner of the Welcome screen and click on it:

That will open the PowerPoint Options dialogue box. On the General tab under the section Personalize Your Copy of Microsoft Office, there is a dropdown for Office Theme where you can choose the theme you want:

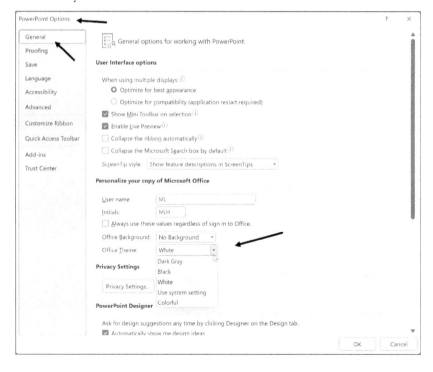

Your other option is to click on Account in the bottom left corner of the Welcome screen. That will bring up the Account page which will also have a dropdown option for Office Theme:

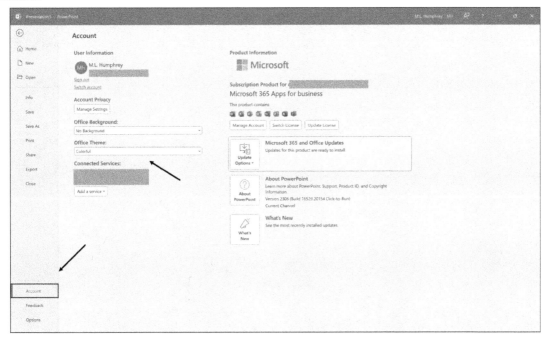

Click on that dropdown arrow and choose the theme you want to use.

Easy enough. Now let's cover basic terminology so that we're on the same page about what to call things.

Basic Terminology

Most of the terminology I use is consistent with Microsoft's Help and what others use, but some of it may be unique to me, so even if you think you know these terms, it's a good idea to at least skim this section anyway.

Tab

I refer to the menu options at the top of your PowerPoint workspace as tabs. This is because in older versions of Office when you selected an option at the top of the screen it looked like a file tab. In more recent versions of Office they've eliminated that appearance so that now the selected tab is simply underlined.

Here you can see the default tab options in PowerPoint:

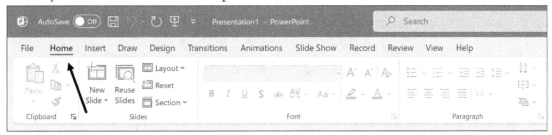

The Home tab is currently selected which you can see because it is underlined. The other tab options listed there are File, Insert, Draw, Design, Transitions, Animations, Slide Show, Record, Review, View, and Help. At times in PowerPoint there will be additional tabs visible when you have certain objects selected.

Each tab has its own set of available options that are grouped together in sections.

For example, as you can see here, the Home tab includes the Clipboard section that has tasks such as copy, paste, and format paint. It also has a Slides section that includes tasks such as add a new slide, reuse a slide, change a slide layout, etc.

When instructing you on how to do something, I will tell you to go to X section of Y tab and then click on Z task. So, for example, go to the Slides section of the Home tab and click on the dropdown arrow for New Slide.

Click

If I tell you to click on something, that means to move your cursor over to that option and then use the mouse or trackpad to either left- or right-click. If I don't say which, left-click.

Left-Click / Right-Click

Left-click simply means to use the left-hand button on your mouse or to press down on the left-hand side of your track pad. (For me on my track pad, it's the bottom of the track pad, but I think some have those buttons at the top instead.)

A left-click is generally used to select something.

Right-click simply means to use the right-hand button on your mouse or to press down on the right-hand side of your track pad.

A right-click generally brings up a dropdown menu of additional options.

Left-Click and Drag

If I ever tell you to left-click and drag this just means to go to that selection, left-click and hold down that left-click while moving your mouse or cursor until you've selected all of the text, images, etc. or until you've moved that selected object to where it needs to go.

Select or Highlight

Before you can make changes to your text, such as size, font, color, etc. you need to select the text you want to edit. If I ever tell you to select text, that means to go to one end of that text, and then left-click and drag to the other end so that the text is highlighted. Like here where I have selected the text "bullet point" in the second row:

- This is a bullet point
- This is another bullet point
- This is another one

Selected text should be shaded like in the image above.

Another way to select text is to click at one end of the text you want to select, hold down the Shift key, and then use the arrow keys to select the text you want. An arrow to the right or left will select one letter at a time; an arrow up or down will select all letters between that point and the same point in the line above or below.

You can select multiple sections of text by selecting the first one normally and then holding down the Ctrl key as you left-click and drag to select the next section of text.

To select an object in PowerPoint, left-click on it. When an object is selected, there will be circles around the perimeter of the object, like this:

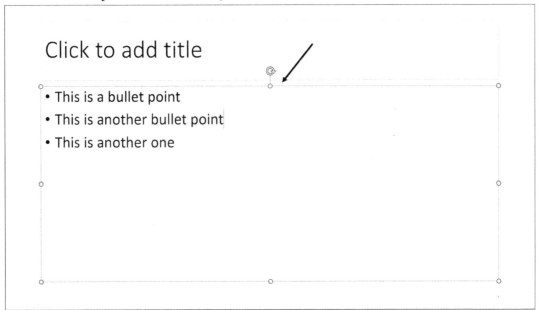

You can see that the second text box in the image above, which contains the bullet points, has been selected, because there are white circles at each corner and in the middle of each edge. Compare that to the text box above that which includes the "click to add title" text where just a faint outline is visible.

We are not going to do much with objects in this book, but I did want to mention it so you know what it looks like.

To select more than one object, click on the first object and then hold down the Ctrl key as you click on the others one at a time.

Ctrl + A, which is a control shortcut which we will define in a moment, can be used to Select All. If you are clicked into a specific text box and you use it, you will select all of the text in that text box. If you are not clicked into a specific text box, then Ctrl + A will select all of the objects on the page.

Dropdown Menu

Often there will be additional choices available if you right-click somewhere in PowerPoint. For example, if you are clicked into a text box of a presentation slide and you right-click, you will see this list of choices that let you cut, copy, paste, etc.:

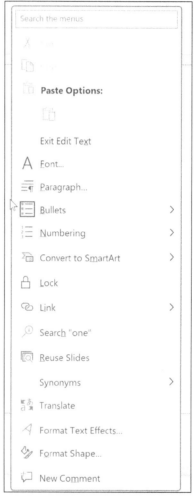

I refer to this additional set of options as a dropdown menu even though sometimes it will actually drop upwards instead of downwards.

Dropdown menus can also be seen if you left-click on any of the arrows for the options under the tabs in the top menu section. For example, here is the Layout dropdown menu from the Slides section of the Home tab:

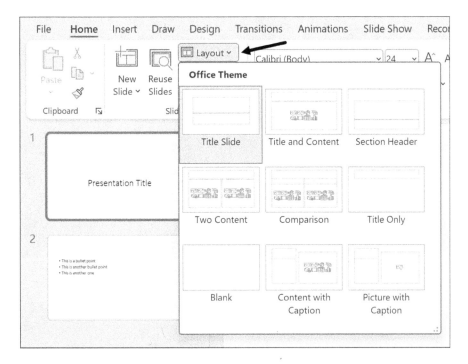

I clicked on the arrow next to Layout which brought up nine slide layouts to choose from. Anytime you see a little arrow like that next to a listed task or below it, that means there are more choices available.

Expansion Arrow

Another way to see more options in that top menu is to click on the expansion arrows that are sometimes visible in the bottom right corner of various sections. You can see one in the corner of the Clipboard section in the image above, for example. Clicking on an expansion arrow will either open a dialogue box or a task pane.

Dialogue Box

The old-school way for Office programs to show you additional options was to use dialogue boxes. Dialogue boxes appear on top of the workspace and can be left-clicked and dragged around. They are usually where you can find the most comprehensive set of options.

If you click in the bottom left-corner of the Font section of the Home tab, you can see the Font dialogue box, for example:

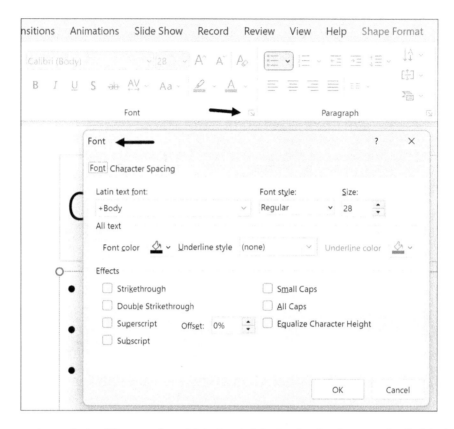

The Font section of the Home tab, which is visible in the background of this image, has options for font, font style, font size, font color, underline, and more. But the Font tab of the Font dialogue box includes those options as well as other options like double strikethrough, superscript, subscript, small caps, and all caps.

To close a dialogue box, click on the X in the top right corner.

Task Pane

In newer versions of Office, they tend to use what I refer to as task panes. These are separate work spaces that are visible to the sides or sometimes below your main work area.

To see an example of a task pane, right-click on a slide and choose the Format X option. It's likely going to be Format Text Effects or Format Shape depending on where you clicked.

This will open a task pane on the right-hand side of the workspace, like this one for Format Shape:

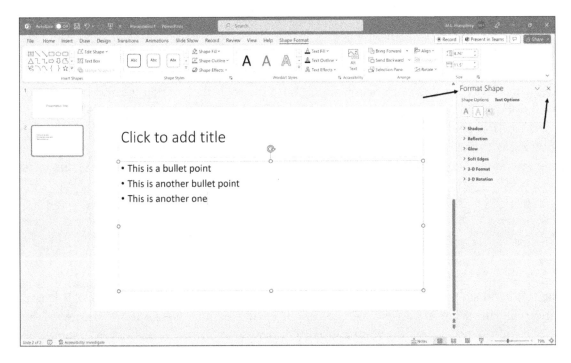

Task Panes usually have multiple sections. You can see above that this one has Shape Options and Text Options. Text Options is currently selected and has three available options to choose from, each one represented by an image with an A on it. The middle one of those is currently selected and that gives the choices of applying Shadow, Reflection, Glow, Soft Edges, 3-D Format, or 3-D Rotation to the text on the slide.

To close a task pane click on the X in the top right corner.

You can also left-click and drag to undock a task pane and move it around if you don't like the default location. To re-dock a task pane, left-click and drag to the side until it once more becomes a part of the workspace. Be careful doing this, because the task pane will reopen wherever you left it last.

Note in the picture above that there is also a sort of task pane on the left-hand side of the workspace, too, for thumbnails of the slides in the presentation. But that area can't be closed or moved. You can resize it, though, by holding your mouse over the inner margin until you see an arrow that points left and right and then left-clicking and dragging the border of the pane until it's your desired width. Note that doing this will impact the size of your slides in your main workspace, too.

You can resize any task pane that way. Just find the inner edge of the pane and then left-click and drag.

Mini Formatting Menu

If you were working in PowerPoint and following along with me, then you've also noticed something I call the mini formatting menu. It's not something I use much because it didn't exist when I was learning all these programs, but I did recently find that it came in handy when I was working on a smaller screen where the top menu options were minimized or hidden.

To see the mini formatting menu, either select some text or right-click in the main workspace. If you right-click, the mini formatting menu will appear above or below the dropdown menu of choices. If you select text it will likely appear above your text, like this:

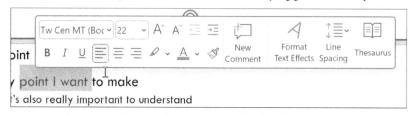

The left-hand side of the mini formatting menu includes the most common text formatting options like font, font size, font color, etc. and is fixed, meaning those options are always there.

The right-hand side of the mini formatting menu is dynamic. It will have default options like those you see here until you start working in PowerPoint, at which point those options will change to be ones you used recently.

That dynamic nature is why I don't use it often, because I'm never sure if the option I want will be there. But for basic formatting, especially if working on a smaller screen or in a tab other than the Home tab, the mini formatting menu may be the best choice.

Scrollbar

To navigate between slides in a large presentation and or through a large list of options in a dropdown menu, you will need to use scrollbars.

Here I've zoomed the main workspace so that you have scrollbars visible on both the right-hand side and the bottom. (Usually a full slide is visible so you won't have a scrollbar on the bottom.):

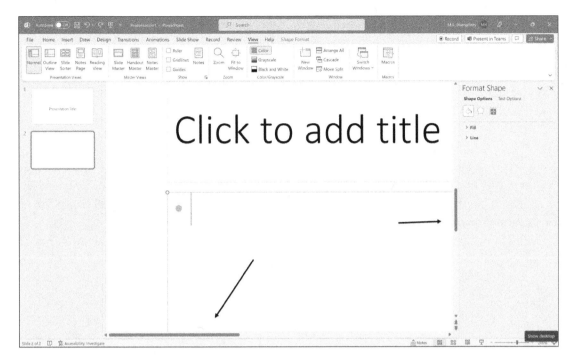

Note the dark gray bars indicated by the arrows. Those are the scrollbars. Or what I call scrollbars.

You can left-click and drag the bar itself to move quickly. In a dropdown menu, like the one for fonts, you will be able to see the choices as you do this.

In your main workspace, you will not see where you are until you let up on the left-click. But if you are scrolling down through your presentation slides it will show a small box that says "Slide X of Y" where X will change as you scroll.

(For me, scrollbars are not the best way to navigate through a presentation. I prefer to click on the slide thumbnails on the left-hand side of the workspace. But I do often need to scroll through that section when I have more than a handful of slides. That scrollbar though lets me see the slides as I do so.)

Another option for working with scrollbars is to click in the lighter-gray space around the actual bar. This will move you in that direction. So if you click in the light gray space above the right-hand scrollbar it will move you up, for example. Or if you click in the light gray space to the left of the bottom scrollbar it will move you left.

If you don't want to move that much at a time, you can also click on the arrows at the very ends of where those bars are. If you use the single arrows to navigate through your slides they will move you one line at a time if you're zoomed in or a slide at a time if you're zoomed out. The double arrows in the bottom right corner of the slide section will move you up or down one entire slide at a time regardless of zoom level.

Slider

Some options in PowerPoint use a slider, which is a horizontal bar with a perpendicular line along the bar that marks the percent value currently being used. You can see in the bottom right corner of your PowerPoint workspace the slider for your zoom level, for example. Click along that bar to change the value.

Control Shortcut

A control shortcut is when you hold down the Ctrl key (or sometimes another key) and then the specified letter to perform an action. So if I write Ctrl + C, that means hold down the Ctrl key and the C at the same time.

I will always write the shortcuts using a capital letter, like I just did, but you don't need to use the capitalized version of a letter. Just hold down that combination of keys at the same time.

Undo

This isn't really a definition, but I want you to learn it as soon as possible. If you ever do something and then regret it, Ctrl + Z will undo the last thing you did. For a more in depth discussion on using Undo and its counterpart Redo, see the Other Tips and Tricks chapter.

* * *

Okay, now let's walk through the absolute basics of working in PowerPoint, including how you open, save, and delete PowerPoint files.

Absolute Basics

Open PowerPoint

There are a number of ways to open PowerPoint. One of the easiest is to double-click on a PowerPoint file. That will open the file and PowerPoint at the same time.

Another is to go to the Start menu (bottom left corner of my screen but may be different for you) and left-click. That will bring up a large dropdown menu with pinned or recently used programs, like here where you can see PowerPoint in that first row:

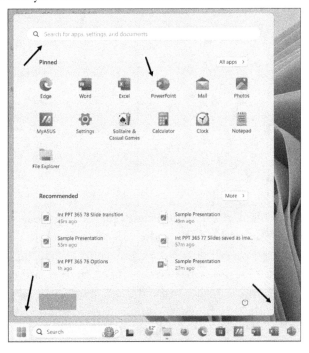

If it's there, just left-click on it.

Otherwise, use the search bar above that to find it. (As of now. They're always changing those options around a bit but the general concept stays the same. You should always see common programs and there should always be a search option somewhere.)

What I like to do is pin my most-used programs to my task bar. In the image above you can see the PowerPoint icon on the right at the bottom of the screen. Every time I need to open PowerPoint I just click on that.

To pin a program to your task bar, right-click on the icon from the start menu and choose Pin To Taskbar. You can also click and drag a shortcut to the program down to the taskbar.

Start a New Presentation

If you open PowerPoint without going through an existing PowerPoint file, you should by default open to the Welcome screen:

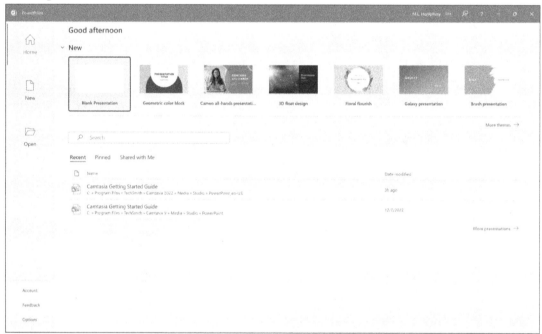

To start with an absolutely blank presentation that's just white slides with black text, click on that Blank Presentation option under New at the top of the screen.

If you're brand new to PowerPoint, I'd recommend doing this and then choosing a presentation theme from the Design tab, because those themes are easier to work with and provide a template for a more basic presentation. However, on the Welcome screen PowerPoint does also provide a number of fancier pre-formatted themes you can choose from. You can see six of those in the screenshot above.

There's also a More Themes option at the far end of that row. Click on that to see even more choices:

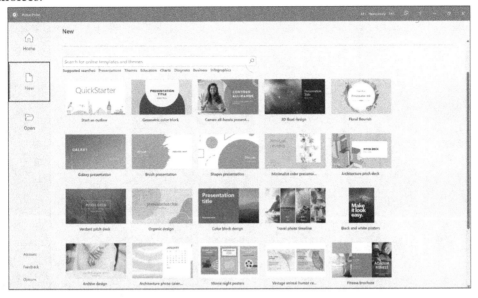

(In the image above, I scrolled down a bit to show more of the templates.)

Here we have twenty options to choose from as well as some Suggested Searches options up at the top that will give you even more choices.

To use one of those templates, click on the applicable thumbnail. PowerPoint will open a dialogue box that talks about the intended use for that particular presentation theme. Click on Create if you want to use it:

Office will then download the template for you and then open a presentation that has a number of slides visible and pre-formatted using that theme:

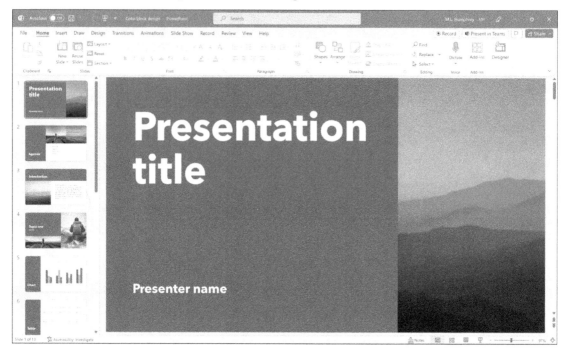

From there you can customize the presentation using your own text and images, which we will spend most of the rest of this book discussing.

If you didn't want to use that template, while you still have that dialogue box up and before you click on Create, as long as you were working from the More Themes screen you will have arrows on the left or right side of that dialogue box that you can use to move through the other template options.

* * *

If you already have a presentation open, the easiest way to start a new presentation is to use Ctrl + N. That will open a plain black and white presentation. You can then either go to the Design tab and choose a theme from there or click on one of the cover slide images in the Designer task pane that will open on the right-hand side of the workspace:

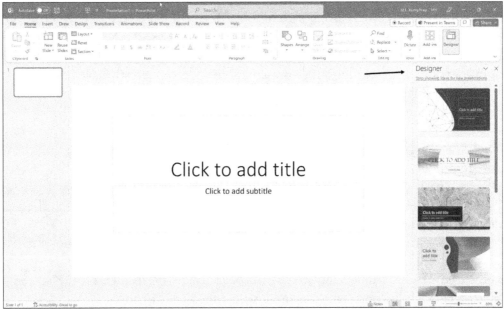

Note that the choices on the right-hand side in the Designer task pane are just a cover slide and not a fully-built template. So by default the accompanying slide layouts are going to be pretty generic. Most just have a colored background, as you can see here on the left-hand side menu of Layout choices:

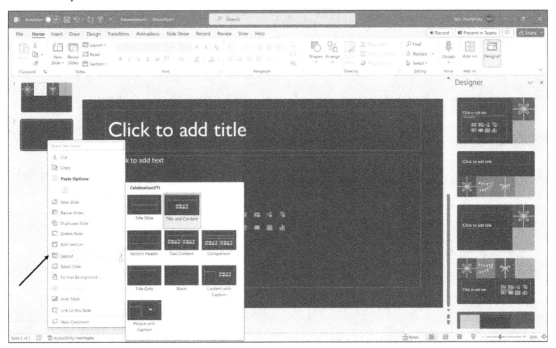

However, you can keep choosing slide layouts from the Designer task pane if you want something more interesting. As you can see on the right-hand side in the image above, Designer continues to suggest various options for each new slide layout.

Your other option for starting a new presentation when you already have one open is to go to the File tab, which will take you to the Welcome screen, and to then choose one of the presentation thumbnails from there as discussed above.

Open an Existing PowerPoint Presentation

There are two basic options for opening an existing presentation. First, go to where the file is saved and double-click to open it. Second, open PowerPoint first and then choose your presentation from there.

For the second option, if you're already working in a PowerPoint presentation, click on the File tab to get back to the Welcome screen. Otherwise, just open PowerPoint.

Your recent PowerPoint presentations will be listed in the center of the screen under Recent. Left-click on the one you want and it will immediately open.

If the file you want is not listed, you can click on Open on the left-hand side of the Welcome screen. This will bring up the Open screen which looks like this:

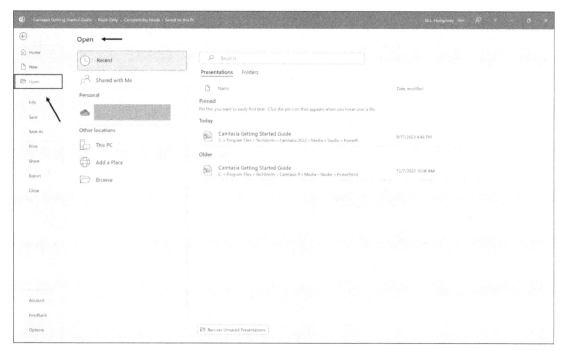

The Open screen will show a listing of your recently-opened presentations and pinned presentations on the right-hand side, but it will also have a section to the left of that where you can search on OneDrive, This PC, or click on Browse for the old familiar Open dialogue box:

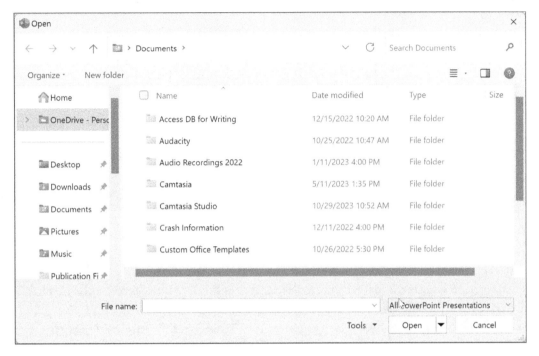

(Note here that the color of that dialogue box is going to depend on your Windows settings. I have changed my background image to a light-colored image which makes this box appear gray. When I have my default background image up instead, this dialogue box is black.)

To use the dialogue box, click on one of the folders in the left-hand side or double-click on a folder in the main section to navigate to where your file is saved. Once there, either double-click on the file you want to open, or click on the file and then click on Open at the bottom of the dialogue box.

The Open screen also has a Folders option up top that you can click on if the file you want is not one you recently opened but is in a folder you recently used. That will display a list of folder names. Click on one to see its contents and then keep clicking through to find your file. You can use the upward pointing arrow next to the file path name above the search box to go back up one level if needed:

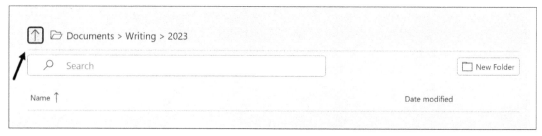

Another option for opening a file from within PowerPoint is Ctrl + O which will take you to the Open screen.

Pin a File

If there are any presentations that you always want to be able to access quickly, you can pin them. (You can also pin folders in the same way.)

To pin a file the first thing you need to do is open that presentation. That will put it into your recent list.

Once the file is showing on the Open screen, move your cursor to the right-hand side of that listing near where the date modified is, and you'll see a pin option appear. Hold your mouse over it and it will say, "Pin This Item To The List".

Click on that pin. The file will move to the Pinned section of your files listing and will show with a pin:

In the Open screen, pinned files are visible at the top of your file listing. In the Welcome screen you need to click on the Pinned option to see your pinned files.

To unpin a file, just click on that image of a thumbtack/pin next to the file name.

To pin a folder, it works the exact same way. Make sure the folder is listed, hold your cursor over that spot, click on the pin, and done.

Save a File

To save a file you have a few options.

Ctrl + S is one of the easiest if you want to keep working on the file. There's also a small icon of a computer disc in the top left corner that you can click on. If the file has already been saved before, that's all you need to do. PowerPoint will save over the latest version of the file using the same name and in the same location.

If the file has not been saved before and you use Ctrl + S or click on that save icon, you will see the Save This File dialogue box:

There will be a default name displayed in the File Name box. It will already be highlighted, so just start typing to give the file the name you want to use instead.

Below that it will have a default location. For me it's my Users file of my C Drive. If that's fine, you just click on Save at the bottom of the dialogue box.

But if you want to use a different location instead, you can click on that dropdown arrow and choose from the listed options. Or you can click on More Options in the bottom left corner. That will take you to the Save As screen:

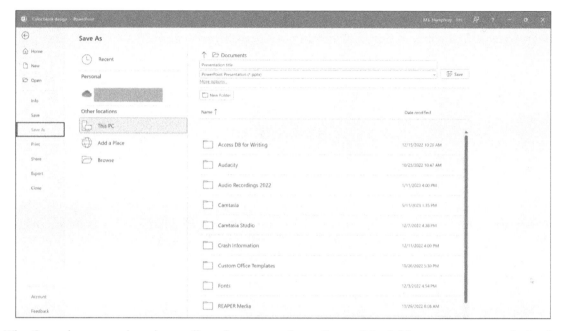

The Save As screen is going to list a larger number of possible folders to save to and also let you change the file type if you need to do that.

You can click on Browse from the Save As screen to bring up the Save As dialogue box which will also let you choose a location, name, and file type.

For most presentations that have been saved before, you'll just save using Ctrl + S or that icon in the top left corner. You can even just close the presentation and when PowerPoint asks if you want to save your changes say yes.

But there are going to be times when you want to save a file with a different name or different format. When that happens, click on the File tab and then click on Save As on the left-hand side of the Welcome screen. From there you can change whatever you need to change.

Do be careful though about changing things this way. If you just wanted to move a file to a new folder, it's better to do that outside of PowerPoint. Same with renaming the file. Let's talk about that now.

Move a File

If you want to just move a file from Folder A to Folder B, that is best done outside of PowerPoint. Close the file, go to the folder where it is saved, select that file, Ctrl + X to cut it from its current location, go to where you want the file to move, and Ctrl + V to place it in that new location.

Keep in mind that if you move a pinned file or a file that was in your recent files list, you will no longer be able to open it from those lists in PowerPoint, because PowerPoint will go to the old location looking for the file and it won't be there anymore. (Same goes for when you change the name of a file.)

Rename a File

If you want to change the name of a file but don't want multiple versions of the file to exist, that should also be done outside of PowerPoint. Find the file where it is saved, click on it to select it, click on it again to make the name editable, and then make your name change. Hit Enter or click away when done.

Delete a File

Deleting a PowerPoint file also needs to happen outside of PowerPoint. Find the file where it's saved, right-click and delete. Or click on it and choose the trashcan or delete option at the top of the dialogue box.

Close a File

Okay. Back to PowerPoint.

The easiest way to close a presentation is to click on the X in the top right corner of the PowerPoint workspace. If you had a single presentation open that will also close PowerPoint.

If you have multiple presentations open that should just close that presentation.

If the presentation you try to close has unsaved changes, PowerPoint will ask if you want to save those changes before closing:

Save will save those changes with the same name, file location, etc. and will replace the prior version of the presentation.

Don't Save will close the file without keeping any of your changes from this session.

Cancel will keep the file open. Choose Cancel if you're not sure and want to review the document before closing it or if you want to use the Save As option to save a new version and keep the old one untouched.

To close a file you can also go to the File tab and then choose Close from there.

Or you can use Ctrl + Q to both save and close a presentation or Ctrl + W to just close a presentation.

Personally, I like to be reminded that there were changes made to my presentation before I close it so I'd avoid using Ctrl + Q, because it never fails that you realize you didn't want to save those changes about three seconds after you automatically save them. But it's there if you want to use it.

* * *

Okay. Those were some of the absolute basics of working with files in PowerPoint. Next let's discuss how to choose a presentation theme from within a new presentation and then we'll cover the layout of your workspace.

Presentation Themes

We've touched on these a bit already, but I wanted to devote a full chapter to presentation themes, because as a new user of PowerPoint I highly recommend working with an existing presentation theme. They often come with a variety of slide layouts that are already formatted for you, and they tend to have nice accent elements that a plain, black and white presentation doesn't have.

We already covered the themes available on the Welcome screen, but I don't recommend those for new users. They're a little too fancy and it's a little too easy to get stuck trying to adapt one to what you need as a new user.

Instead, I recommend that new users start with the black and white presentation option and then go to the Themes section of the Design tab:

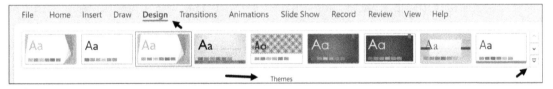

You can see here the current theme as well as eight other choices. In the bottom right corner of that row, there is a downward pointing arrow with a line above it. Click on that to expand your list of choices.

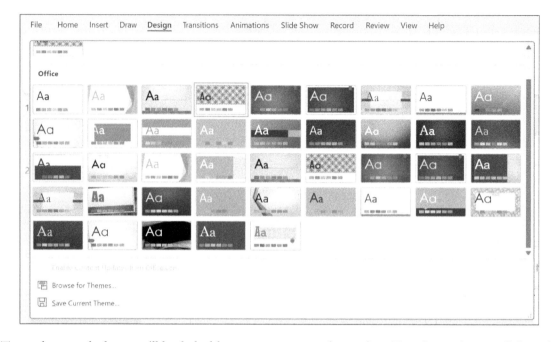

To see how each theme will look, hold your mouse over the option. To select a theme, click on it.

The nice thing about using one of these themes is that moving back and forth between them is relatively easy. You just click on the one you want and everything updates.

Many of the theme choices in this section also have variants. You can find them in the Variants section of the Design tab after you click on a theme.

So here, for example, the Facet theme has a green, a blue, and a pink option as well as a version that uses a dark green background:

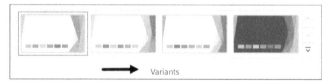

There is also a Colors dropdown that you can find if you expand the variants section. Expand that section and then hold your cursor over Colors and a secondary dropdown menu will appear with a large list of color combinations to choose from.

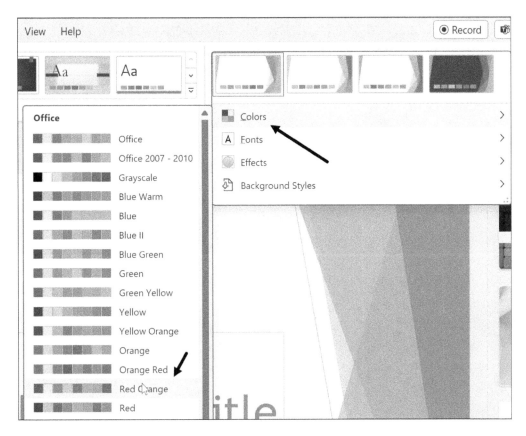

Click on the color combination you want to use. Above, for example, I applied a Red Orange color palette to the Facet theme and you can see in the background that the accents and text changed to match that choice. (In print, maybe not, but in the ebook you can see that.)

For a beginner, I think there's plenty here to work with and it's pretty forgiving, too, so I strongly urge you to use one of these themes for your presentation if you don't have a corporate one you need to use.

The problem I found with using the themes currently listed on the Welcome screen is that when you try to change to a theme in the Themes section of the Design tab, at least for the few I tried, PowerPoint didn't completely change over. It combined the two themes, and not always in a good way.

As a beginner, I wouldn't expect you to be able to unravel that. So to avoid that potential complication, I'd say just start with a blank presentation and then choose an option from the Design tab.

(This is different, by the way, than earlier versions of PowerPoint where the Welcome screen choices corresponded to the Themes options on the Design tab. So it may change back in the future. But for now, save yourself the heartache.)

Also, even though they don't show up by default when you choose a theme, all of these older design choices do come with a variety of built-in slide layouts that use those colors and design elements. Here, for example, Facet has fourteen different slide types for you to choose from.

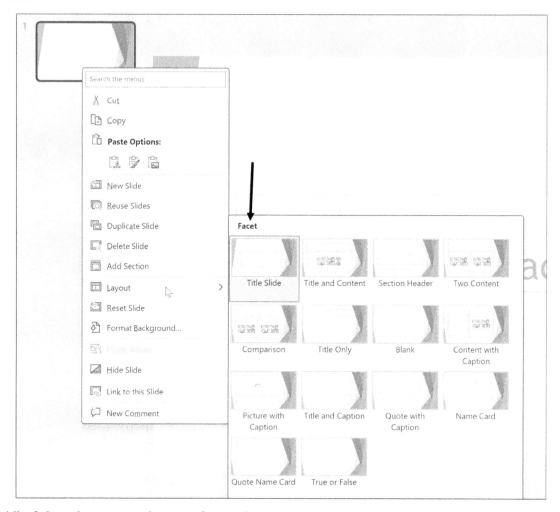

All of those layouts use the same font, color, and accent elements to help you create a cohesive presentation. Is it sexy? Nah, not really. Is it functional? Yes.

Okay. So that's my advice. Open a black and white presentation, choose a theme from the Design tab, and change the color if you want to be adventurous.

But. When you open a black and white presentation, PowerPoint is also going to open the Designer task pane on the right-hand side. Like so:

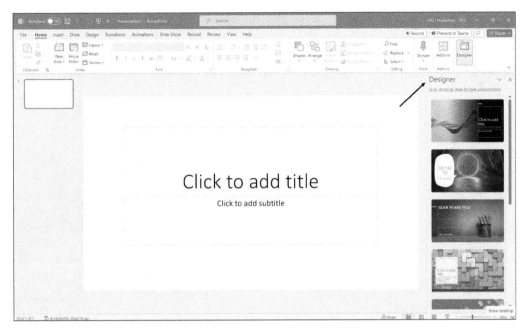

My advice is to ignore it. Click on the X in the top right corner and pretend you never saw it.

But if you're tempted...you can click on one of those options in the task pane and PowerPoint will apply that design to your title slide. If you're lucky it will also offer you some good layout options for other slides in your presentation.

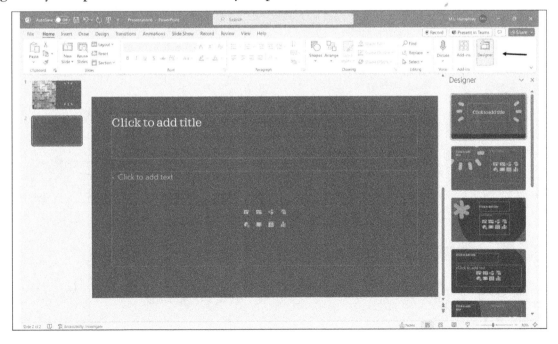

If you're not, you'll get options like this:

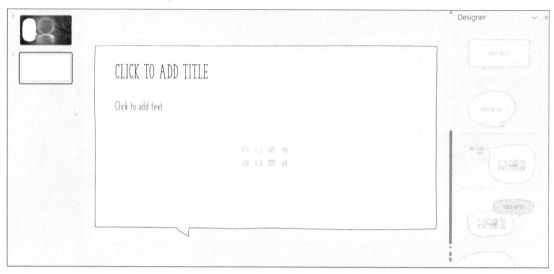

And switching over after you've made that choice is not easy to do. Best to just close the presentation and try to start again instead of try to choose another option.

Now, I understand that you may not be thrilled with using those basic presentations in the Themes section of the Design tab. Another option to make things more interesting, is to start with one of the basic themes, add a new slide (we'll cover how to do that soon), and then open the Designer task pane to see more layout choices than the default. Like these:

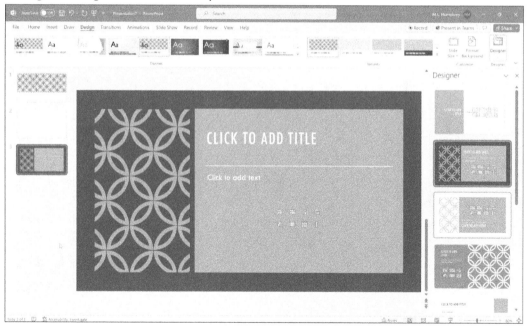

To open the Designer task pane, click on Designer in the Designer section of the Design tab, which you can see in the top right corner of the image above.

I think that gives workable options that are maybe a little more interesting than the default and that still work thematically. You can also switch to a new theme without PowerPoint trying to combine the two designs, although be forewarned that you'll probably have to go through each slide and choose a better layout option.

So that's probably your best call. Start with a blank presentation (Ctrl + N or click on that option on the Welcome screen), apply a theme from the Themes section of the Design tab, choose a variant or color option, if wanted, and then click on Designer to give yourself more choices for your slide layouts.

But only click on Designer after you've added at least one slide to your presentation, don't use it on your title slide.

And one final note. If you move to a new theme after you've added text to your presentation, be sure to check all of your slides. Sometimes there will be a difference in font size or font choice that impacts your appearance. Also be especially careful if you were using a theme that had all caps in the title sections and you move to one that uses upper and lower case. I often find that I didn't properly capitalize my words when all caps was in place.

One more thought. If you are going to print your presentation, try to find a presentation theme that has a white background on the main slides. Like this one:

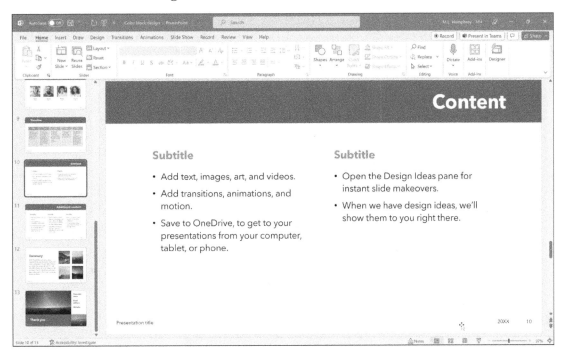

It is possible to set your print settings to address slides with dark backgrounds when it comes time to print, but I always prefer that my presentation on the screen match what I've printed.

The reason not to print slides with a dark background is that it takes a lot of ink. And sometimes, depending on the type of printer, a dark background has more chance to smear or smudge or come through stripey.

Also, make sure the theme you choose has layouts that meet your needs. Are there section slides if you need that? Are there image slides? What about the bulleted lists, do they work for you? It's far easier to start with a theme that is set up for your needs than to try to edit it later. And in this beginner book we're not going to cover too much about how to make those sorts of edits, so you're going to be stuck with how the theme is set up.

Okay, now let's look at your workspace.

Your Workspace

This is what PowerPoint looks like using a presentation that has about a dozen slides:

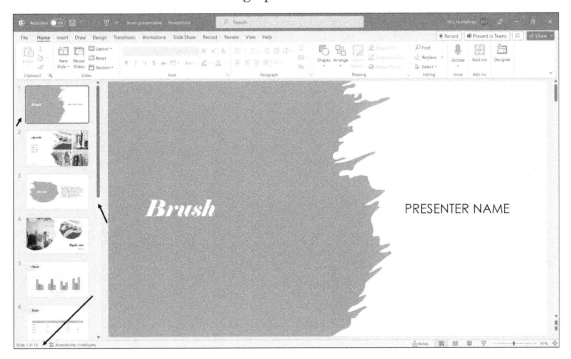

As discussed previously in the definitions section, across the top of the workspace are the tabs, File, Home, Insert, etc. You can click on each of those to see the available options and then click on an option to apply it.

Below that, on the left-hand side of the workspace, are thumbnail images of each slide. You can see six slides at a time at the current size. On the bottom left corner it shows that there are a total of 13 slides in this presentation. The scrollbar for that section is on the right-hand side of the thumbnails, and can be used to move down to see the rest of the slide thumbnails.

To the right of that is the main part of the workspace where you can see the current slide and then to the right of that is another scrollbar.

There is a slider in the bottom right-hand corner of the workspace that will let you zoom in or out on the current slide. My default zoom percentage is 97% which usually lets you see the entire slide while keeping the slide thumbnails visible on the left-hand side. I tend to leave this on the default setting but you can click down there to change your zoom level quickly.

In the image above, I am clicked onto Slide 1. You can see this in the left-hand set of thumbnails where there is a darker border around Slide 1 and the number of the selected slide is also a different color.

To move to a different slide in the presentation, either left-click on a slide thumbnail in the left-hand section, or use the scrollbar on the far right of the currently-visible slide. In that far right scrollbar the double arrows in the bottom right corner will move you one slide at a time regardless of zoom level.

As you work in PowerPoint you may end up opening other task panes which will appear on the right-hand side of the current slide or below it. Or even to the left if you change your settings. But what you see above is the core appearance that you'll see most often.

Now let's walk through what you can do with those slide thumbnails on the left-hand side.

Slide Thumbnails Task Pane

As we just discussed, the left-hand side of your workspace shows thumbnail images of each slide in your presentation. This is where you go to add, delete, or move around your slides in your presentation.

Add a Slide

If you want to add a slide to your presentation, there are a few options available to you.

You can right-click on the slide directly above where you want to add that new slide and choose the New Slide option from the dropdown menu:

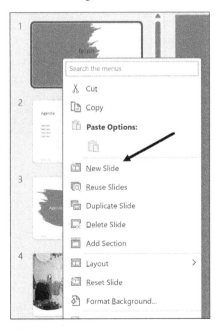

That will add a blank slide that corresponds to the template you're using. The layout used will vary depending on the slide that was directly above.

Here I right-clicked on the top slide for this presentation style and chose New Slide and it added a slide in the default layout for this template as Slide 2. But then I also did the same on what is now Slide 3 and it added a new slide in the same layout as Slide 3 as Slide 4:

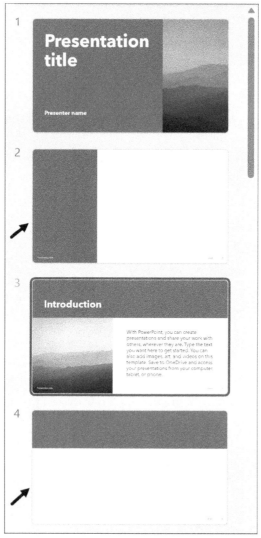

So. The layout you'll see on your new slide is going to vary depending on where you insert the slide and what layout was being used above that. (But, as we'll discuss momentarily, you can easily change that.)

Another option for inserting a new slide is to go to the blank space at the very end of the Presentation Slides Task Pane and right-click on that space. Choose New Slide from there and

PowerPoint will add a slide to the end of your presentation using the same layout as the last slide.

Your final option is to go to the Slides section of the Home tab and click on New Slide. If you use the dropdown arrow under New Slide, you can choose the layout you want:

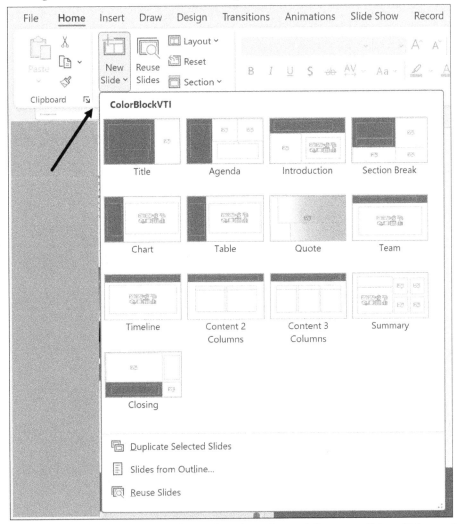

Simply click on your preferred layout from that dropdown. The new slide will insert below the slide you currently have selected in the presentation. If no slide is selected, it will insert at the end of the presentation.

Select Slides

To select a single slide, just left-click on it.

To select multiple slides, left-click on the first slide, and then either hold down the Shift key or the Ctrl key and select the next slide.

Use Ctrl if you want to select one additional slide at a time and also if the slides you want to select are not next to one another.

Use Shift to select a range of slides. With Shift, you left-click on the first slide in the range, hold down Shift, and then left-click on the last slide in the range. All slides between the two slides you clicked on will then show as selected.

Selected slides have a darker border around them and the number of the slide is also a different color. Here I have selected slides 1 through 3:

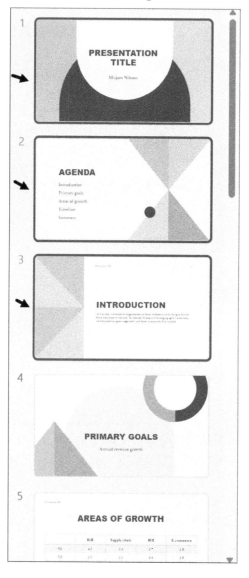

I clicked on Slide 1, held down Shift, and then clicked on Slide 3. (I could have also held down Ctrl and clicked on each individual slide, but Shift saves time when you're selecting a range of slides at once.)

You can combine Ctrl and Shift together to select slides. So maybe you use Shift to select three slides that are next to each other and then Ctrl to select one more slide that isn't next to those three.

To go back to just one slide selected, click on that slide.

You can also click into the gray area at the bottom of the task pane if you don't want any slides selected. The slide you'll see in the main workspace in that case will be the last one in the presentation.

If you want to select all of the slides in the presentation, click into the Presentation Slides task pane, and then use Ctrl + A.

Move a Slide or Slides

It's not a problem if you insert a slide in the wrong location. You can easily move the slide to where you need it. You can also move a range of slides at one time.

To move a single slide, left-click on the slide you want to move, and then hold that left-click as you drag the slide to its new location. Release your left-click when you reach your destination.

Here you can see that I've left-clicked on Slide 18 and am dragging it upward past Slide 17:

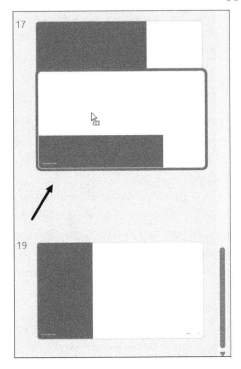

As it reaches a spot above Slide 17, Slide 17 will shift downward to make room for that slide to go above.

To move multiple slides at once, it's basically the same, you just need to select all of the slides you want to move first, and then left-click and drag.

Here you can see that I'm moving two slides (see the red 2 above the outlined slides) and that I've moved those two slides to a spot between the existing Slides 5 and 6 (see the slide numbers on the left-hand side):

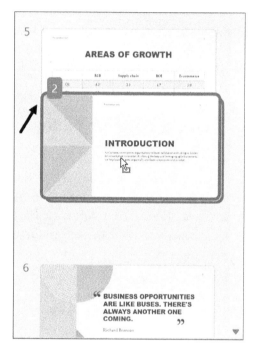

Note that as you moves slides around they will not keep their numbering. The numbering is based on that slide's current position in relation to all of the other slides in the presentation. As soon as you move your slides into their new location, all slides in the presentation will renumber to adjust to their new position.

You can also Cut and Paste a slide to move it. This sometimes is the easier option if you want to move a slide a large number of spaces. To do this, left-click on the slide you want to move, use Ctrl + X (or click on the scissors in the Clipboard section of the Home tab), go to the place in the presentation where you want to place the slide (using the scrollbar on the right-hand side of that task pane if needed), click on the slide above where you want to place the slide, and then use Ctrl + V (or the Paste option in the Clipboard section of the Home tab) to paste the slide into its new location.

Cut can also be used to take slides from one presentation to another. Select the ones you want to move, Ctrl + X, go to the other presentation, and Ctrl + V.

If you want the slides that you paste into the second presentation to use the formatting of that second presentation, then use the Paste dropdown menu in the Clipboard section of the Home tab to choose a different paste option. There are three options to choose from:

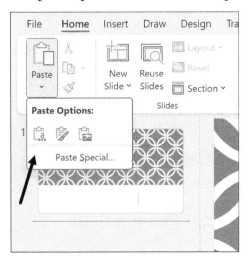

You want the first option, Use Destination Theme.

You can see the description of each paste option if you hold your mouse over the little icon. Right now the Use Destination Theme option looks like a clipboard with an "a" in the bottom right corner with dots under it.

You can also find these paste options when you right-click in the gray space of the Presentation Slides task pane. Either one will work.

Cut, or Ctrl + X, takes a slide from where it is and moves it to a new location. But if you want a copy of that slide to move and want to keep the original where it is, then use Copy, or Ctrl + C, instead. Everything else works the same in terms of pasting the slide into its final location, but Copy will leave the original slide where it was.

In the Clipboard section of the Home tab, Copy is represented by an image of two pieces of paper stacked on one another.

(Note that sometimes Microsoft decides they need to refresh the look of their product and changes the appearance of these icons. But they generally stay in the same location. And in twenty-five years they have yet to change the Ctrl shortcuts. So if you know the Ctrl shortcuts you should always know a way to cut, copy, and paste.)

Duplicate a Slide

PowerPoint also has an option similar to Copy which is Duplicate. You can find it by right-clicking on a slide thumbnail or by using the dropdown under the Copy option in the Clipboard section of the Home tab.

Duplicate takes the slide you currently have selected and puts an exact copy of that slide directly below. So it saves that step of having to paste.

It will copy any text or images, etc. that were on the source slide so if a header is going to stay the same or you have other elements that will repeat from slide to slide, it's very useful.

And you can use it on more than one slide. Just select the slides you want to duplicate first and then choose the Duplicate option and all of the selected slides will be duplicated.

Delete a Slide

To delete a slide, right-click on it and choose Delete Slide from the dropdown. This also works with multiple slides at a time.

Another option is to use the Delete key when you have a slide or slides selected. The Backspace key also works to delete a selected slide or slides.

Reset a Slide

If you make changes to a slide and you don't like them and you want to go back to the default format for that theme, you can reset the slide. Right-click on the slide and choose Reset Slide from the dropdown menu or go to the Slides section of the Home tab and choose the Reset option from there.

When pasting in slides from another presentation, even if you pasted in using the destination theme, you may still want to do this. When I just did this with my pasted slides it brought my text to a left-aligned position instead of centered, for example. If I'd already had slides in this presentation that had been created in the presentation, that difference in alignment would have been noticeable and needed to be fixed.

* * *

Next let's discuss how to choose slide layouts.

Slide Layouts

A good presentation will vary the appearance from slide to slide. Maybe one slide will just contain text but then another will have a chart or two columns of text side-by-side. Presentation themes often have these various layouts built in so that you don't have to try to create one on your own.

To change the layout of a slide, right-click on either the slide thumbnail in the Slide Thumbnails task pane or in the main workspace. Next, go to the Layout option. There should be a secondary dropdown menu that shows you the available layouts for that presentation theme:

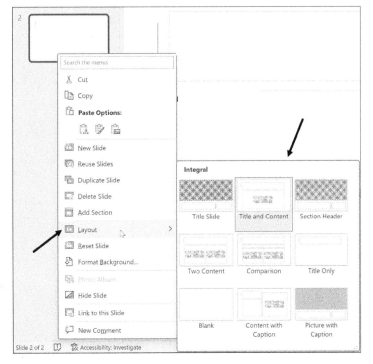

Click on the one you want to use.

You can also do this by selecting the slide and then going to the Layout dropdown menu in the Slides section of the Home tab. Just click on the arrow next to Layout and choose from there.

If you're using the Designer task pane, you can also click on one of the options shown there to apply it. The Designer task pane will not always have suggestions for all slide types, though.

Also, not all themes will have all layouts, so be sure to check what choices you have available before you start working with your chosen theme.

Now that you know how to apply a layout, let's discuss some of the more common choices.

Title Slide

The title slide is the first slide in your presentation. It will usually have a space for a title and a space for a subtitle as well as the design elements for your chosen theme.

Here, for example, is the title slide for the Facet theme:

It places the title and subtitle in the center of the slide.

Other themes will place those elements in different locations. For example, the Frame theme places the title and subtitle on the left two-thirds of the slide.

Section Header Slide

Another common slide layout is the Section Header layout. It usually includes fields for a title and a sub-header:

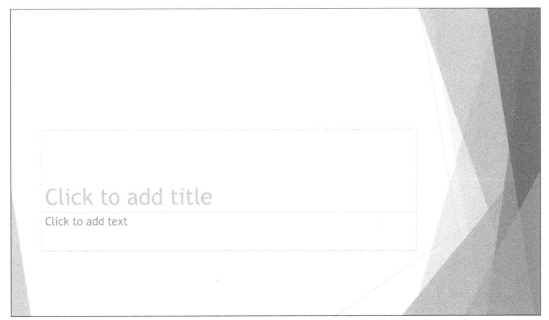

Often-times this will look very similar to the title slide, but maybe the colors on the slide, the font size, or the placement of the text or design elements will differ slightly.

With this theme, the text is on the left of the page instead of centered and the design element in the background is different on the left-hand side.

The Section Header slide is one where you might want to use the Designer to choose different options. In this case there are options with a dark background, like the first and third options here, that make the section stand out more:

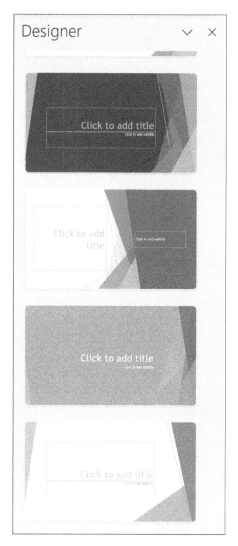

There are also choices that place the text in different locations on the slide, like in the second option.

Remember, if the Designer tab is not visible you can open it by clicking on Designer in the Designer section of the Design tab. Scroll down to see all of your options.

One caution about using the Designer is that the list of slide choices is not going to be the same each time. So if you choose a design that you like for one section header, you'll likely need to duplicate that slide for your next section header to use it again.

Title and Content Slide

The Title and Content Slide is your bread and butter slide. This is the one you will probably use the most. It has a section with the title for the slide, which is usually what that slide is about, and then another section where you can add text or another element like a video, image, illustration, graph, or chart. (We're only going to cover adding text in this book but the Title and Content slide will accommodate any of those other elements, too.)

This theme uses a pretty standard layout with the title at the top and then the text or other element below that. But, as we can see with the Designer choices, that's not the only way to go. Some themes put the title on the left and text on the right like the fourth option here:

Also, if using Designer, be careful, because as you can see here, sometimes the suggested layout doesn't match the type of slide you want, like in the third example there that only has a title.

Two Content or Comparison Slide

A Two Content slide generally has a title section and then two sections with text or other elements side-by-side.

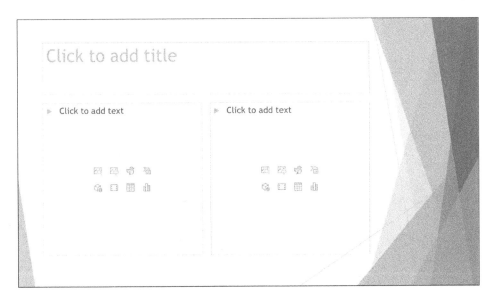

This is one that, at least for this theme, PowerPoint didn't have additional suggestions for in the Designer tab. If I wanted something different then this basic appearance, I'd probably have to build it myself. Not a beginner-level skill.

A Comparison slide layout is much like a Two Content slide, but it has one additional text box above each of the sections in the main body of the slide so you can label those contents.

Content or Picture with Caption

A Content With Caption slide has a title section and an associated text box, and then another box for text or another element like a picture, video, etc.

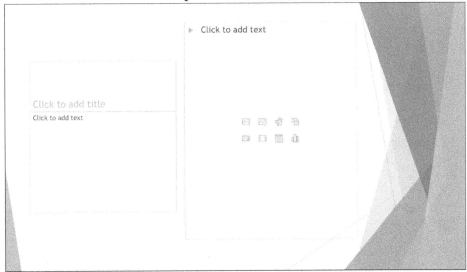

This is a good one for a high-level description, a descriptive paragraph, and then an image, like this:

A Picture With Caption slide is similar but may limit the choice for that third box to just a picture as opposed to text or images. Also, the positioning of the three elements may differ between the two different layouts.

* * *

There are a number of other slide types, but the ones above are probably going to be your core group of slides. Once you've selected a theme to work with, you can look at the layout choices and see if any of them will fit for what you want to do. For a basic presentation, you should be fine no matter what theme you choose.

Okay. Now that you know the basics about working with your slides and applying a layout to them, let's talk about how to add and format text, which is usually the core of creating a PowerPoint presentation.

Add, Move, or Delete Text

Add Text

It's very easy to add text to a PowerPoint slide. Find a text box, click on it, and start typing. That's why I recommend using the theme templates, because they already have text boxes for you and they're generally located in good spots on the slide.

So, how do you know where a text box is? Simple. They usually say something like "Click to add title" or "Click to add subtitle". Like here:

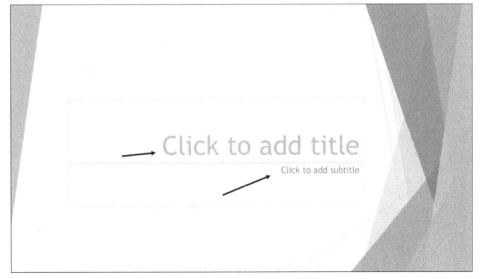

You can see the boundaries of the text boxes with that faint gray line around the edges. The current text color, font, and size is what your text will look like when you click into the box and start typing.

You don't have to replace that text "click to add…" because it will disappear as soon as you click into the text box. (If you already had text in a text box, then, yes, you would have to delete that text to get rid of it, but not this placeholder text.)

When you're done typing your text into the text box, click away from it. The outline of that text box will go away and you'll just have your text. Like so:

All slides work this way. Some, though, are going to have bulleted lists. Like this one:

In that case, when you start typing and hit Enter for a new line in that main text box, it will put bullet points at the start of each line. Use the Tab key to indent a line of text and create a multi-level bulleted list. Like so:

> A Really Important Point
>> No, seriously, very important
>>> The most important point of all
> A Second Really Important Point
>> But maybe not as important as the first one

To enter this text, I clicked into the text box, typed the first line, hit Enter, used Tab, typed the second line, hit Enter, and used Tab again before I typed the third line of text. That gave me the first three lines.

I then hit Enter and used Shift + Tab twice to move the bullet point back to the first level, and then added that line, Enter, Tab, and then the final line of text.

So with bulleted lists, Tab will move the bullet point in one, Shift + Tab will move it back one. It's easiest to do as you type, but if you need to make adjustments later, click into the line of text right before the first letter, and then use Tab or Shift + Tab as needed.

Another option is to click anywhere on a line and then go to the Paragraph section of the Home tab and use the Decrease List Level or Increase List Level options:

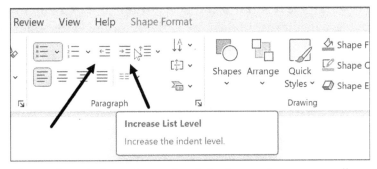

In this template, the various indented text levels had text that was smaller with each indent, but the bullet point remained a green arrow. In other templates the type of bullet point used may change with each level.

As a beginner, I would suggest letting PowerPoint set those shapes and text sizes. These templates tend to be built for use as a presentation that will be shown on a projector screen, so they won't use too small a font size to be visible in that setting. See here how the text in the last three bulleted lines is the same:

> A Really Important Point
>
> > No, seriously, very important
> >
> > > The most important point of all
> > >
> > > > It really is
> > > >
> > > > > I'm not lying
> > > > >
> > > > > > This is really, really, really important

One final comment, if you're working in a company presentation template and having issues with the bulleted lists not working, that's probably an issue in the master slide of the template, and you'll need someone to fix that or you'll need to switch to a different template or presentation theme. So sometimes it's not you, it's them.

Move Text

You move text in PowerPoint in the same way you would in Word, which I hope you're familiar with already.

Select the text you want to move, and then use Ctrl + X or go to the Clipboard section of the Home tab and click on the scissors to cut the text from its current location. Next, click on where you want to place that text, and then use Ctrl + V or the Paste option in the Clipboard section of the Home tab to place the text.

You can also select the text and then right-click and choose Cut from the dropdown menu, go to where you want to place the text, right-click, and choose Paste from the dropdown menu.

Copy Text

Usually you'll want to move text not copy it, but you can copy using Ctrl + C, the Copy option in the Clipboard section of the Home tab, or by right-clicking and choosing Copy from the dropdown menu. Just select your text first. The text will remain where it is, but you can then also go to a new location and paste that text there as well.

Paste Options

As mentioned above, there is more than one paste option. Either click on the arrow under Paste in the Clipboard section of the Home tab or right-click to see the list of paste options.

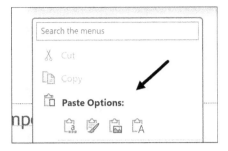

We already discussed the first option there, Use Destination Theme. That makes sure the text fits in with what's around it in terms of font, color, etc.

The next one is Keep Source Formatting which will paste the text in but keep it the same color, font, etc. that it was when you copied it.

The third option, Picture, pastes the text in as a screenshot. The text won't be editable at that point. It will be as if you'd taken a photo of that text and dropped in the photo.

The final option, Keep Text Only, will format the text depending on the text that's around it.

Here's an example of all four options:

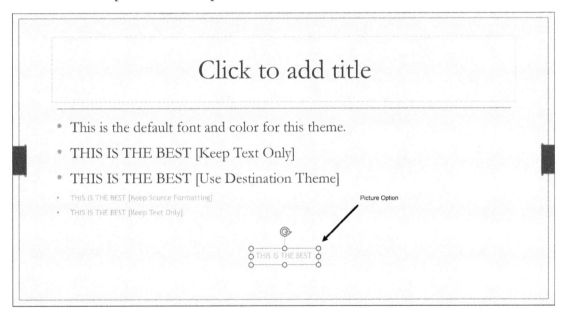

My source text was in green and used the Trebuchet MS font. The presentation I'm pasting into uses the Garamond font in black, like in that first bulleted line there.

In the second bulleted line, I pasted in "THIS IS THE BEST" using the Keep Text Only option. I did the same thing for the last line of text. Note how different they are.

That's because the first line was pasted directly after a line that had black text in Garamond and the second one was pasted directly below a line that had green text in Trebuchet MS.

Each one used the formatting of the text immediately before it.

The third bulleted line in the image above was pasted in using Use Destination Theme. No matter where I pasted that text in within that text box it was going to look like that.

The fourth line is that same text pasted in using Keep Source Formatting. It continues to look like the text I initially copied, which was green and in Trebuchet MS font.

Finally, down there in the center bottom you have a picture of the text I was copying and pasting. I can't edit the text in that last one, it's a picture at this point. And it doesn't position like text anymore either. I have to click and drag that image around to place the text on my slide. But that is a true image of what the source text I started with looked like.

Delete Text

To delete text, select the text, and then use Backspace or Delete.

If you don't select the text first, you can remove text one character at a time. Delete will delete the character to the right of your current position. Backspace will delete the text to the left of your current position.

Delete and Backspace also work on bullet points and the numbers in numbered lists.

Design Principles

Feel free to ignore this section. I have given a number of presentations to various audiences over the years and been on the receiving end of even more, but at the end of the day I have no formal design training, this is just what I've picked up in my finance/consulting/corporate career.

Font Size

For a presentation that is going to be given as an actual presentation, I prefer to keep the font size to 14 pt or higher. You want people to be able to see what is on your slide.

Even though most of the templates will go down to 12 pt, I figure if I'm getting that deep into subpoints, I can probably break the idea down better across a couple of slides.

Note that this rule goes out the window if it's a consulting-style presentation deck that is meant to be printed and handed out. In that case, I'd still recommend 8 pt or above and only use 8 pt for footnotes.

Font Size Consistency

Sometimes PowerPoint automatically adjusts the size of your text to make it visible in your text frame. For example, in the template I've been using for the screenshots for this book it took my text from 36 pt to 32 pt when I tried to have a title section with three lines in it.

Why should you care? Because it can be noticeable during a presentation if five slides are at 36 pt and then one slide is at 32 pt. Or if all of your bulleted points are at 18 pt and 16 pt and then suddenly there's a slide that's at 12 pt.

I will sometimes manually adjust my slides for that lowest common denominator (32 pt or 12 pt in the examples above) to keep the appearance consistent from slide to slide. (We'll cover that soon don't worry.)

Hierarchy of Elements

You want there to be a natural hierarchy among your elements. The font size of the title of a slide should be bigger than the main body text. And any subpoints should be the same or a smaller font size than the main points.

Also, at least in the U.S., the natural tendency is to start at the top and go downward and to start at the left corner and move towards the right. So top-left is usually where you should put whatever you want the audience to see first.

And when placing any other elements, like images or tables, etc. they should be below and or to the right of the text that introduces them.

Font Type

For most of the text in a presentation the goal is for it to be legible. Use workhorse fonts like Times New Roman, Garamond, Arial, etc. Also, if you're in a corporate setting know what the approved corporate font is and use that.

Summary Instead of Detail

When presenting to an audience you don't want to just stare at your slide and read it. You also don't want your audience to be so busy reading your slide that they don't listen to you.

Ideally, to avoid those problems, you will list one line per thought on a slide and then expand on that thought verbally. The text on a slide is more of a framework to work from, not everything you ever wanted to say about the topic.

Now, I will note that consulting presentation decks don't work this way. On those they seem to put every single thought they've ever had and then everyone sits around reading the slide instead of listening. It's almost like a written report in PowerPoint form. Consultants like them because they can still walk through the slides as if they're a presentation and rack up those nice billable hours. (Why, yes, I am jaded.)

Keep It Simple

Later we'll walk through animations and we're going to talk about how to change font colors, etc. But always keep the goal in mind, which is usually to convey information to your audience. If flying, spinning, whirring text helps you do that? Great, use it. If something like that will make your audience stop listening to you, then don't use it.

Same with colors and themes and everything else. Always ask yourself, "Does this help me get the message across?" If not, nix it.

Better to be boring and convey your message than have people talk about all the animations on your slides and forget what the presentation was about.

Contrast

There is a reason that black text on white backgrounds for generic products was so popular at one point in time. Because it works. Black on white, very legible. Very easy to see the words. Red on black? Not so much.

Red on green? Don't go there. Some people are red-green colorblind. Others are blue-yellow colorblind. That means they can't see the difference between certain colors, like blue and purple. So if you put blue text on a purple background, you maybe lose 8% of your audience right there.

Black text on a white background really is the best. Be creative in your headers and design elements, but make sure your main text is as legible as you can get it.

Make It Make Sense

We're not going to cover things like SmartArt in this introductory book, but when I do cover it in the intermediate book one of the things we will discuss is that you need to choose graphics that work for what you're trying to say. If you have connected arrows pointing to the right, your audience will expect that the first element on the left happens before or leads to the next element and so on and so forth. Don't use a graphic like that for unrelated points. Or list the points out of order. None of this:

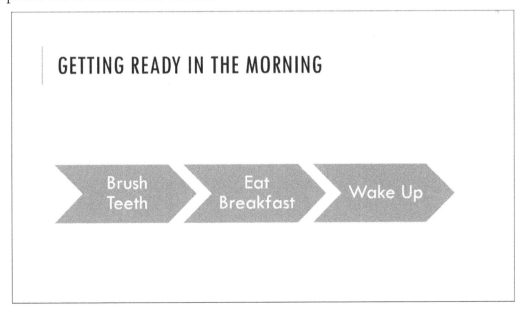

You may brush your teeth before you eat breakfast, but you certainly don't do both of those before you wake up. Right? Always make sure your graphics in your presentation make sense.

* * *

Okay. Now let's discuss how to format your text.

Format Text Basics

There are four primary options for formatting text. With each you need to select your text before you try to use it.

The first is control shortcuts for common formatting like bold, italics, and underline.

The second, the one I use most often, is to go to the Font section of the Home tab and choose from the options listed there.

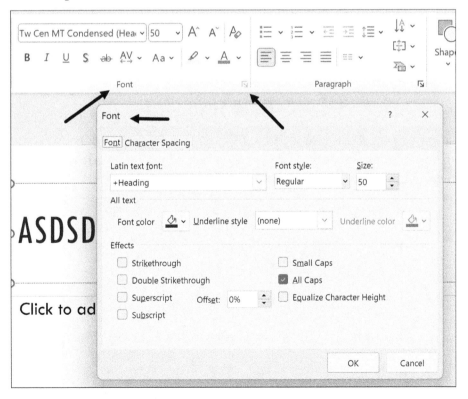

The third is to open the Font dialogue box. To do so, either click on the expansion arrow in the corner of the Font section of the Home tab (see the arrow pointing to the left in the image above) or right-click and choose Font from the dropdown menu.

Both options will open that dialogue box that you see above. Apply the formatting you want from there.

The fourth option is to use the mini formatting menu. If it doesn't appear when you select your text then right-click to bring it up along with a dropdown menu. Choose your formatting option from there.

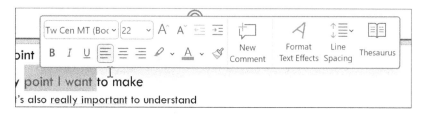

* * *

Now let's walk through all of your formatting options alphabetically. That will make this an easier section to refer back to later.

I am going to assume here that you have already selected the text you want to format, so I don't have to tell you to do that each time. Note that an easy way to select all of the text in a text box is to click into the text box and then use Ctrl + A.

Bold Text

The easiest way to bold text is to use Ctrl + B.

You can also in the Font section of the Home tab or the mini formatting menu, click on the bolded capital B in the second row of options:

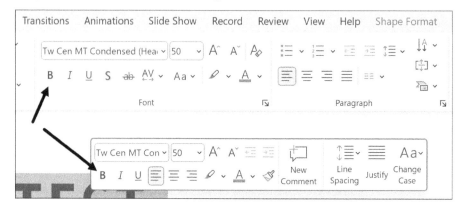

Or in the Font dialogue box you can change the Font Style dropdown to either Bold or Bold Italic, depending on which one you want.

To remove bolding from text, you do the same thing. Select the text and then use Ctrl + B, click on the B in the menu, or change the Font Style in the Font dialogue box to Regular.

If you have text that is both bolded and not bolded and use either Ctrl + B or the B in one of the menu options, you may have to use it twice to get the result you want. It will take all of the text in one direction—bolded or not bolded—and if you were trying to go in the other direction, then you have to use Ctrl + B or the B in the menu one more time. The Font dialogue box does not have this same issue since you're specifically telling Excel which formatting you want to apply.

Font

Fonts are what dictate how your text looks. In the paste examples above, we saw the difference between a serifed font (Garamond) and a sans-serif font (Trebuchet MS).

When choosing a font, keep in mind readability. There are some nice, tried and true fonts that are used often for written documents because they work. Garamond and Trebuchet are two of them. Times New Roman and Palatino are a couple others.

If you work for a company, they may have a corporate font that they've designated for all of their communications. If that's the case, use that one.

You can either change your font before you start typing, or select all of your text afterwards and change it then.

Both the mini formatting menu and Font section of the Home tab have a dropdown menu for font where each font's name is written in that particular font so you can see what type of font it is:

By default, your font list is probably going to look like the list above. Those little clouds with arrows in them mean that if you want to use that particular font you need to download it from Microsoft.

(You can turn this off if you want so that only available fonts are shown. To do so, go to File, then choose Account in the bottom left corner, and click on Manage Settings under Account Privacy. Scroll down to the Connected Experiences section and uncheck the box for Turn On Experiences That Download Online Content. Another option is to uncheck the box that's a little further down that says Turn On All Connected Experiences.)

Back to the font listing.

At the top you'll see any fonts that are used by the theme in your current presentation. Below that you'll see any recently-used fonts. And then after that you'll see an alphabetical listing of all available fonts.

Usually, I'm trying to use a specific font. In that case, click into the field with the current font name and start typing. As you type the font name, Microsoft will autopopulate the name for you. When it lists the font you want, you're good, just click away.

For example, I just clicked into that field and typed "Ti" and it changed the value to Times New Roman for me. All I had to do was click away and my selected text updated to the new font.

If you're not quite sure of the font you want, but know the basic name, you can start with the dropdown menu open and then start typing the font name you want in that field. The dropdown menu will jump to that part of the alphabet and you'll be able to see all choices in that range and click on the one you want from the list.

I will note that PowerPoint was a little weird for me just now when I tried to type in a font name I didn't have. When I clicked away into the presentation, PowerPoint brought up a dialogue box where it tried to name the current font what I had just typed. If that happens to you, click on the No option and it will go away.

You can also use the Font dialogue box to choose a font. Use the Latin Text Font dropdown menu to do so. You won't be able to see the difference between the options there though, and I don't think it gives any additional functionality, so I never use it.

Font Change Case

To change the capitalization of a text selection, you can use the Change Case option available in the Font section of the Home tab. It's the option in the bottom row with an Aa and a dropdown arrow.

Your choices are Sentence Case, Lowercase, Uppercase, Capitalize Each Word, and Toggle Case. You can see in the screenshot below an example of each one applied to the text "this is sample text. and one more sentence. Last one."

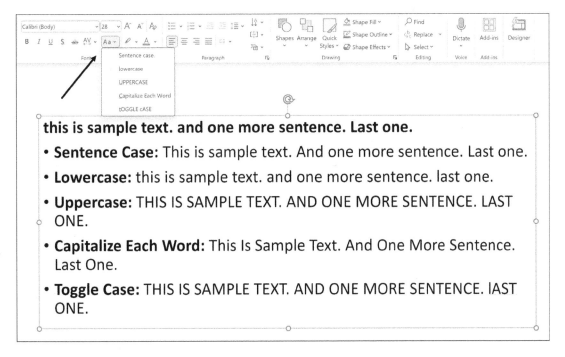

Sentence case capitalizes the first letter in the first word of each sentence. Uppercase puts everything in all caps. Lowercase puts everything into lowercase. Capitalize Each Word changes the first letter of each word to a capital letter. Toggle Case flips the capitalization for every single letter.

For the lowercase and Toggle Case examples, the changes in the above image are subtle. For lowercase, you have to look at the L in the last sentence which is no longer capitalized. And for Toggle Case you have to realize that everything was capitalized except for that last L which was put into lowercase.

In the mini formatting menu, Change Case is not always going to be one of the available choices.

The Font dialogue box only gives you All Caps, which is the equivalent of Uppercase. It does also have Small Caps as an option, though, which I sometimes use in tables of contents or header sections.

Font Color

Both the Font section of the Home tab and the mini formatting menu have an A with a red line (at least initially) under it that allows you to change the color of your text. Click on the arrow next to the A to see sixty possible colors to choose from:

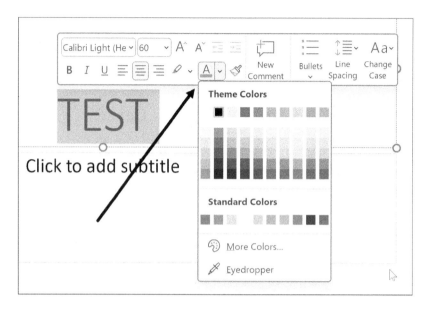

If you see a color you like, click on it to apply it.

In the generic presentation template your color choices are going to be the standard color choices you see in Word or Excel. There are shades of black and gray as well as columns for shades of blue, orange, yellow, and green along with a set of ten Standard Colors that are basically bright rainbow colors.

But here is that same dropdown when I'm in a presentation that has an assigned color scheme:

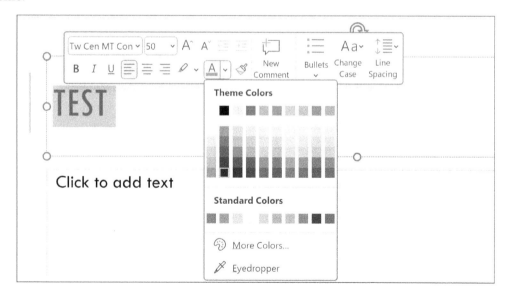

In this case, the Standard Colors and the first three black and gray columns of choices are the same, but then the other seven columns of color choices tie to the colors used in the theme. Which means if you choose one of those colors it's liable to work well with the other colors in the presentation. (Sorry if you're reading in print, you won't see that, but you can try it for yourself in PowerPoint.)

Sometimes, of course, you will need to use a specific color. For example, I have worked for employers who had assigned colors for their brand and all communications had to use very specific shades of each color.

In that instance, click on the More Colors option to bring up the Colors dialogue box. It has a Standard tab and a Custom tab, which look like this:

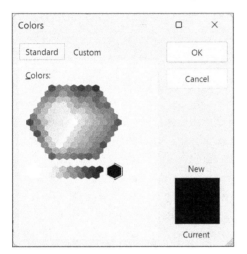 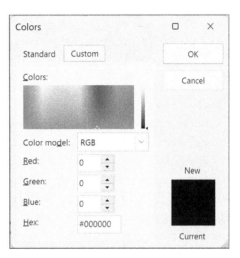

Click over to the Custom tab if you have RGB, HSL, or Hex code values for the color you need to use. Enter the relevant numbers, click on OK, and there you go.

The Font Color dropdown has one more option, the Eyedropper. Click on that option if you have an image or something else in your PowerPoint that uses the color you want. Your cursor will turn into an eyedropper when you do that.

You can either hold the cursor over your selection and it will show you the RGB values for that color, or you can click directly on the color you want to use and it will place that color in the Recent Colors section of the Color dropdown menu. Once you've grabbed the color or the value, it works the same as any other color.

The Font dialogue box also has the same color options but no Eyedropper.

Font Size

To change the font size, I usually go to the Font section of the Home tab, click on the dropdown arrow next to the current size, and select a new value:

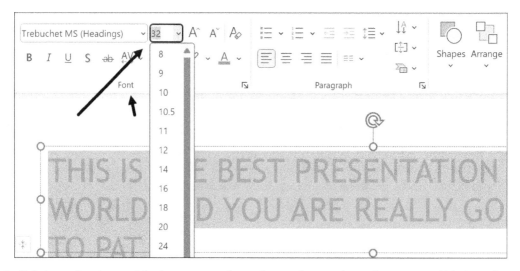

Or I click into that box with the current font size and type the value I want if it isn't listed in the dropdown.

(If you ever select a range of text where the text is of varying sizes, the size you'll see in that font size field will show as X+ where X is the smallest font size in the selected range. So, 12+ for example where the size of the selected text ranges from 12 pt to 20 pt.)

Another option that I never use, but that you may want to use, are the increase font size and decrease font size options that are located to the right of the font size dropdown menu.

There's a bigger capital A with an up arrow and a smaller capital A with a down arrow. Click on either of those to change the font size one step up or down, respectively. The dropdown menu lists the font sizes that are used. So a 12 pt font will go up to 14 pt or down to 11 pt, for example.

These same options are also available in the mini formatting menu.

The Font dialogue box has a Size field. Click into the field and type in a new value or use the up and down arrows to change the font size by .1 pt at a time.

Italicize Text

The easiest way to italicize text is to use Ctrl + I.

In the Font section of the Home tab or the mini formatting menu, you can also click on the slanted I in the bottom row. It's between the options for bold and underline.

In the Font dialogue box, change the Font Style to either Italic or Bold Italic.

To remove italics from text, you do the same thing. Select the text and then use Ctrl + I, click on the slanted I in the menu, or change the Font Style in the Font dialogue box to Regular.

Keep in mind that if your text is mixed italics and regular text and you use an option other than the Font dialogue box, you may need to use the option twice.

Text Direction

By default the text in your presentation is going to be horizontal left-to-right. But there are other options available for text direction, namely rotated 90 degrees, rotated 270 degrees, and stacked. You can find this setting in the top right of the Paragraph section of the Home tab. The dropdown menu there lets you choose which option you want:

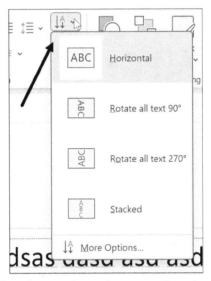

For text boxes, all of the text box has to share the same direction. So if you want different text to use different directions on the same slide, you need to use separate text boxes for each one.

Next to each option you can see a sample. So Rotate All Text 90 degrees turns the text so it runs downward and you'd have to tilt your head to the right to read it. Rotate All Text 270 degrees rotates it in the other direction so you have to tilt your head to the left. Stacked puts one letter per line but doesn't change how the letters are angled.

Clicking on More Options will open the Format Shape task pane on the right-hand side of your workspace, but the Text Direction dropdown menu there has the same four choices.

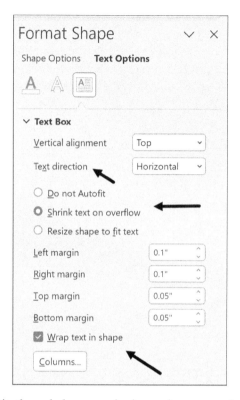

You may still want to use it though because it does give you a few other choices, including whether or not to Autofit your text to the text box, whether or not to shrink the text if it overflows the text box, and whether to resize the text box to fit the text.

This is also where you can say whether the text should wrap to a new line when it hits the edge of the text box.

Underline Text

For a basic, single-line underline the easiest choice is Ctrl + U. You can also click on the underlined U in the second row of the Font section of the Home tab or the mini formatting menu.

If you want more underline options than that, you need to use the Font dialogue box. As of now (late October 2023), there are sixteen underline options available there in the Underline Style dropdown:

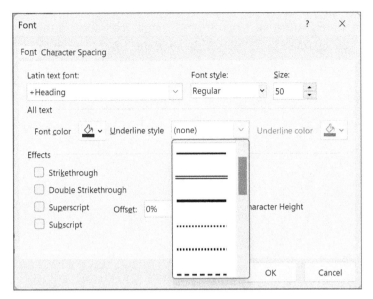

You not only have a double underline choice, but also various dotted, dashed, and wavy line choices. Make your choice and then click OK to close the dialogue box and apply the change.

To remove an underline, you do the same thing again. For Ctrl + U and the U option in the menus, it will either remove a basic underline or transform a non-basic underline to a basic underline. Which means if you used a non-basic underline and try to remove it, you may have to use Ctrl + U or the U in the menus twice to do so.

For the Font dialogue box you just choose the none option from the dropdown menu.

As with italics and bolded text, if the text you select is both underlined and not underlined, you may have to use the Ctrl + U or the U option in the menus two times to get the result you want.

* * *

Clear Formatting

One final note. If you are working in a presentation that uses a theme—so has standardized fonts, colors, etc.—and you change your text away from that, but then later decide you want to go back to the standard look for that presentation, you can use the Clear All Formatting option in the top right corner of the Font section of the Home tab to do that.

* * *

Finally, if you look at the Font section of the Home tab you'll see that there are a few other formatting choices listed there such as strikethrough, character spacing, and text shadow. We're not going to cover them in detail in this beginner book, but they work the same. Select your text, click on the option you want to use, and done.

Format Paragraphs

The last chapter covered the basics of formatting individual letters or words. But sometimes the changes you need to make are at a higher level, the paragraph level or above. So that's what this chapter is for.

As with formatting text, my go-to is the Home tab. There is a Paragraph section there that has all of the options we're going to discuss here and a few more.

Sometimes an option may also be available in the mini formatting menu, but not all of them and not as consistently as with the font options.

You can also right-click in your workspace and choose Paragraph, Bullets, or Numbering from the dropdown menu, as needed. Paragraph brings up a Paragraph dialogue box while Bullets and Numbering both have secondary dropdown menus that let you choose the bullets or numbering to use.

One difference between text formatting and paragraph-level formatting is that you don't have to highlight all of the text to make a change if you're formatting a single paragraph. Just click somewhere in the paragraph and then apply the change you want.

Okay. Let's dive in and walk through some of these options.

Bulleted Lists

Many of the themes in PowerPoint come with bulleted lists already set up. So you bring up a Title and Content slide and you can see immediately that when you add text it will be bulleted. Like here with the Ion Boardroom theme:

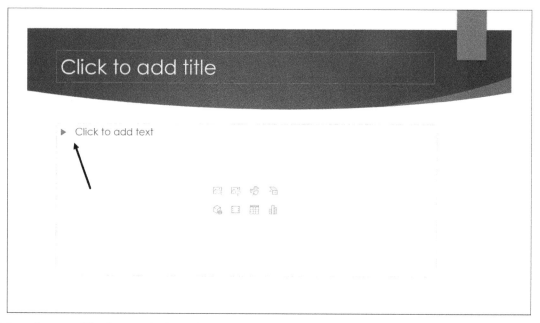

Other themes, like Integral, don't have a bulleted list built in or use one that doesn't have a visible marker. So if you want a visible marker for those themes you have to add it yourself.

To do this, option one is to add the bullet before you start. Click into that text box on your slide, go to the Paragraph section of the Home tab, and click on the dropdown arrow for Bullets:

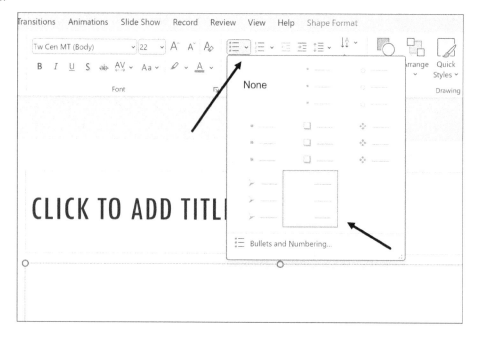

As you can see in the image above, this theme is using a bullet style that doesn't have a shape to it, so to a viewer it's as if there isn't a bullet. To change that, click on one of the six choices you can see there that do use a bullet. If you want there to be no bulleted formatting at all, click on None.

Once you do that, you'll see a grayed-out version of the bullet type you chose and when you start to type it will appear as a fully-colored bullet on the slide.

Here you can see one line of text that I already typed with the bullet fully visible. But since I haven't started typing on the second line that second bullet is grayed out:

When you choose the type of bullet before you start typing, PowerPoint automatically defaults to creating a bulleted list for you. Each time you hit Enter, it will put a bullet at the start of the next line. If you don't want that, use the Backspace key to get rid of it.

Option two is to wait until you're done. Enter however many lines of text, select them all, and then choose your bullet type. PowerPoint will insert your chosen bullet at the left-hand side of each new line of text you entered.

Above I applied bullets by using the Paragraph section of the Home tab, but as I mentioned earlier, you can also right-click and use the secondary dropdown menu under Bullets:

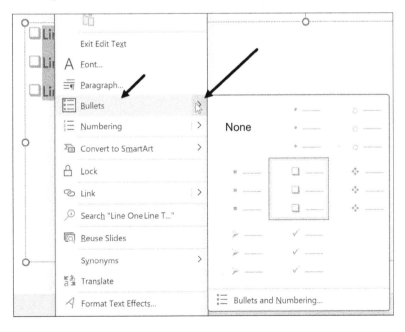

If you click on the Bullets and Numbering option under that dropdown, it will open the Bullets and Numbering dialogue box, which lets you also control the size and color of the bullet:

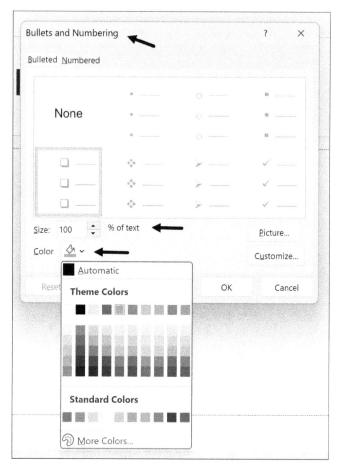

For most bulleted lists, when you hit Enter and then use Tab that will indent the next line of text and use a different bullet either in terms of size or type. You can change from that default, but if you do you may end up having a lot of manual formatting to do each time you want an indented bullet point.

(I'm assuming here that you will not try working with a master slide to make that change.)

This is probably easiest understood if we look at an example:

⬜Default 1
⬜ Default
⬜Default

⬜Default 2
○ Changed Bullet
○ Carried Through Change
○ Carried through change

○ Carried through change

The first three lines here are what the default looks like if I use the shaded box bullet. Each time I indent, the bullet style stays the same, but it gets smaller.

The next four lines I made a change to the first subpoint. I changed the bullet used there to a circle. That then carried through to the next line and also to the subpoint after that next line. Which, all good.

But then…When I tried to create a new main point there at the bottom, it continued to use the circle shape.

So now that final line doesn't match the bullet point used on the other two main points. To fix that, I'd have to manually change it back. And then if I had a subpoint under that, I'd have to change that one to use the circle again.

Honestly, for me, not worth the headache. I'd just stick with the defaults. But there are people I have worked for that tend not to be the ones that do this work who do have strong opinions on what they want to see. So if you work for one of those, you may have to do some manual fixes to get the appearance they want.

If your slide is already using one type of bulleted list and you want to change all of the text on the slide to a different bulleted list, or like mine above to just standardize it to one list, click into the text box, Select All (Ctrl + A), and then make your choice in the Bullets dropdown.

Numbered Lists

Another option you have for points in a slide is to number them. I used to work for an employer who liked to use the Harvard Outline Format, for example. (Complete pain to work with—the format—and more money wasted on something insignificant than you can imagine. Consulting does not believe in the KISS principle.)

Alright. So. To create a numbered list, it works much the same way that a bulleted list does, except you want the Numbering dropdown menu:

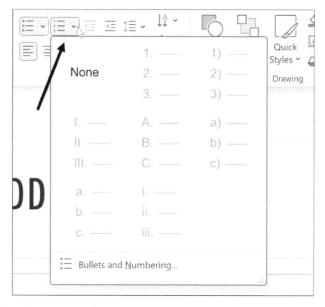

I don't recall this being the case before, but maybe it was. Right now in PowerPoint as I try to create a multi-level numbered list, it just repeats the numbering choice on the next level. Like so:

I. Point 1
    I. Subpoint 1
    II. Subpoint 2
        I. Subsubpoint 1
        II. Subsubpoint 2
II. Point 2

See how I'm using a Roman numeral for the first level? And then it uses a Roman numeral for the second level? And the third? If I want to use some sort of standard outline format, that means a lot of manual edits. Because I will want Roman numeral followed by capital letter followed by standard number followed by lower case letter. And that is not what is happening here.

Good news is I can click onto any of the lines for a certain level under a point and change the numbering choice and it changes the associated lines as well. So it took two clicks and two changes to get this:

```
  I.    Point 1
        A.   Subpoint 1
        B.   Subpoint 2
             1.   Subsubpoint 1
             2.   Subsubpoint 2
  II.   Point 2
```

Now, it's possible you could set up a custom multi-level list in a Master Slide, but that's beyond us. I don't recommend mucking around in Master Slides unless you really know what you're doing because you can really screw things up.

For example, I started working at a new employer a couple months ago and I had to do a presentation, so I grabbed the corporate template we were supposed to use. And someone had borked the thing. You could not get a bulleted list to work at all if it had more than one level. Because someone who didn't know how to work in Master Slides had gone in there and accidentally limited the slide to only one level of bulleted points.

So this is the workaround I'm going to give you instead: If you have to do a multi-level numbered list for a PowerPoint slide, build it in Word. And then copy and paste that list into PowerPoint. It will keep the numbering formats you used in the other program and let you add more lines at each level without an issue.

One final note on numbered lists. Sometimes you will want to start on a number other than 1 or a letter other than A. To make that happen, click into the line you need to change, and then open the Bullets and Numbering dialogue box. (Using either the Numbering secondary dropdown menu when you right-click on the text, or the Numbering dropdown menu in the Paragraph section of the Home tab. Choose Bullets and Numbering from the bottom of either list.)

On the right-hand bottom side of that dialogue box it will say Start At and show a number in a box. Just change the number to what you need it to be. If you're working with letters, then A is equivalent to 1, B is equivalent to 2, etc.

Decrease List Level/Increase List Level

We've already covered one of your options for changing the list level of a point or numbered item. Tab indents or increases the item one level, Shift + Tab decreases it by one level.

But you also have options for this in the Paragraph section of the Home tab. In the top row are options for Decrease List Level and Increase List Level. So if you ever forget Tab and

Shift + Tab, you can always use those instead. They are located directly to the right of the bullets and numbering dropdown choices.

The left-hand one that points to the left is the Decrease List Level option. The right-hand one that points to the right is the Increase List Level option. Just click on your row and use the one you need.

These options are also part of the mini formatting menu.

Specify Amount of Indent

Sometimes you will need to have your text indented by a very specific amount and you won't be able to just use the default formatting in your PowerPoint theme. When that happens, right-click on a line that is at the level you need to fix, and choose Paragraph from the dropdown menu.

This will bring up the Paragraph dialogue box which lets you control Indents and Spacing: You can then change the Before Text value to indent your text the proper amount. Be careful,

Paragraph				?	✕
Indents and Spacing					
General					
Alignment:	Left	⌄			
Indentation					
Before text:	0.81" ⇕	Special:	Hanging ⌄	By:	0.31" ⇕
Spacing					
Before:	2 pt ⇕	Line Spacing:	Multiple ⌄	At	1.07 ⇕
After:	0 pt ⇕				
Tabs...			OK		Cancel

because your changes will only apply to your selected text. Good news is it will carry through to new lines that you add from that point forward for that level. But if you wait to fix this until the end you may have a lot of fixing to do. (Or a lot of format painting to do, which we're about to cover.)

You can also use this setting with a standard paragraph of text that isn't bulleted or numbered if you want the text to sit away from the left-hand edge of your text box.

Format Painter

Sometimes you can save yourself a lot of effort by getting one line or paragraph formatted correctly and then using the Format Painter which is located in the Clipboard section of the Home tab and looks like a paintbrush.

What the Format Painter does is it takes the text color, font, font size, numbering style, bolding, italics, etc. from the text you select, and then applies that formatting to the text you tell PowerPoint to apply it to.

So in our messy bulleted and numbered list examples above, if I get the formatting on one subpoint the way I want it, I can select that text, click on the Format Painter, and then select the next line of text and it will transfer over all of my formatting for me.

At least for numbered or bulleted lists, right now it looks like I can just click into the line that has my formatting I want, click on the Format Painter, and then click on my other line and all of the formatting transfers. I don't have to select the entire line of text.

But if that doesn't work, then you may need to select the whole line of text or paragraph that's formatted the way you want before you use the Format Painter. Sometimes there's a little trial and error involved.

If you have multiple locations where you want to transfer formatting, you can double-click on the Format Painter when you select it. That will keep it turned on until you either click on it again or use Esc to turn it off.

A few cautions about the format painter.

It is a wonderful tool that can save you a lot of effort, but it will apply the formatting to the next text you click on. So be very careful where you click after you turn it on. If you mess up, use Ctrl + Z to Undo, and try again.

Also, at least in Word and I assume in PowerPoint too, sometimes the way you select the text will impact what formatting is applied. I've had situations in the past where I selected a paragraph starting at the top down and the Format Painter didn't capture the formatting I needed. But if I selected that same paragraph starting at the bottom, it did. So if it doesn't work the way you thought, try selecting the sample text in a different way.

If you need the formatting between paragraphs or bullet points to copy over, be sure to select multiple paragraphs or bullet points in your sample.

Also, know that the Format Painter takes *all* the formatting and transfers it, so be careful there. Sometimes it transfers a little more than you want it to transfer.

The Format Painter tool is also available from the mini formatting menu.

Text Alignment

The next significant formatting change that you may want to make at the paragraph level is the alignment of your text. So far we've been looking primarily at examples that are left-aligned with a ragged right-hand margin.

But you can center text, align it to the right, or justify it. This is best understood with a visual example:

> This is a paragraph of text that has to cover multiple lines so we can discuss the difference between the different alignment options. This one is **left-aligned.**
>
> This is a paragraph of text that has to cover multiple lines so we can discuss the difference between the different alignment options. This one is **centered.**
>
> This is a paragraph of text that has to cover multiple lines so we can discuss the difference between the different alignment options. This one is right-aligned.
>
> This is a paragraph of text that has to cover multiple lines so we can discuss the difference between the different alignment options. This one is **justified.**

The first paragraph there is left-aligned. That means that all of the rows of text along the left-hand side of the page are aligned. You can draw a straight line and connect the start of "this", "we", and "options". But note that the right-hand side is not aligned that same way. That's a ragged right-hand margin.

The second paragraph there is centered. Each line is equally distributed around an invisible center line that runs through that space. You can especially see that in the third line of text where there is a lot of space to the left and right of the text in that line.

The third paragraph is right-aligned. In this case, the words on each line all line up on the right-hand side ("so", "alignment", and "aligned") but the left-hand side is uneven or ragged. See how the second line is longer than the first and definitely longer than the third.

The final paragraph is justified. Both the left and right-hand sides are aligned. To make that happen, PowerPoint adds extra space between the words in the line. Usually the difference is so subtle no one notices, but if you use a lot of big words it can become very obvious. With justified the final line is simply left-aligned.

You can choose your text alignment options in the Paragraph section of the Home tab in the bottom row:

Each option is formatted like the choice. So here we have Align Left, Center, Align Right, and Justify. I have my cursor over the Center option in the screenshot above so that you can also see that each option has a control shortcut.

Ctrl + L will left-align, Ctrl + E will center, Ctrl + R will right-align, and Ctrl + J will justify your selected text. (The only one of those I use often enough to have memorized is Ctrl + E to center.)

The left, center, and right-align options are available in the mini formatting menu on the left side on the bottom. The justify option is on the right-hand side and may not always be available.

You can also choose your paragraph alignment option in the Paragraph dialogue box. It has one final option that isn't available elsewhere, Distributed. That is usually not something you'll want. It takes your text and forces it to cover the entire space in the text box even if that means placing large amounts of space between each letter. (This can be helpful for graphic design projects, but if you're creating book covers or something like that in PowerPoint there are far better tools for that out there.)

The text alignment options we just discussed are related to how the text is arranged left to right within a text box, but there are also options for how text is arranged in a text box top to bottom. Again, this is probably best understood with an image:

This is top-aligned text.		
	This is middle-aligned text.	
		This is bottom-aligned text.

On the left-hand side is the default option you'll normally see, top-alignment. The text starts in the top of the text box and as you add more text it will fill in the text box until it reaches the bottom.

The second example there is an example of middle-aligned text. In that instance, whatever text you add into the text box will be placed so that there is an equal amount of space in the text box above and below the text. As you add more text, your text will expand both upward and downward until you fill the text box.

The final example is bottom-aligned text which starts at the bottom of the text box and then fills the text box from the bottom to the top.

Here I've added another paragraph to each one so you can see the difference in how they handle additional text:

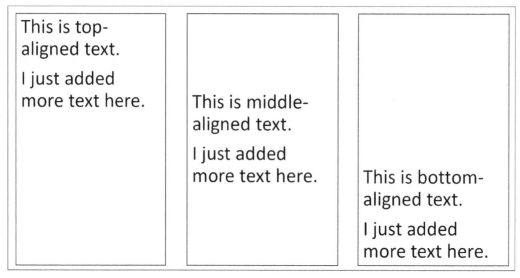

To apply this kind of alignment, click into the text frame, and then go to the Paragraph Section of the Home tab and choose the option you want from the dropdown menu.

The option for this one is a bit buried, at least for me. If you use a bigger screen it might not be as buried for you, but for me it's a tiny little icon on the right-hand side of the Paragraph section of the Home tab. It looks like a box with a line in the middle and arrows pointing up and down. But I can see that it's the one I want because if I hold my cursor over it it says "Align Text". Here it is:

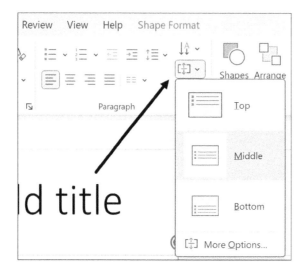

Click on More Options to bring up a Format Shape task pane on the right-hand side of your workspace where you can use the Vertical Alignment dropdown menu to choose Top, Middle, Bottom, Top Centered, Middle Centered, or Bottom Centered. Those last three options combine the Center option with Top, Middle or Bottom.

By default this is not an option available in the mini formatting menu. (That menu is dynamic so if you recently used it then the option may appear for you to select, but since it's not guaranteed to be there, I just skip right past it and go to the Home tab.)

Columns

In the example above I had three separate text boxes to display that text. But if the effect you want is to have your text appear on the page in multiple columns like in a magazine layout, then the best way to do that is to use the columns option with a single text box.

Add your text or click into that text box, and then go to the Paragraph section of the Home tab. The Add or Remove Columns option is in the bottom row and by default shows two sets of lines side-by-side:

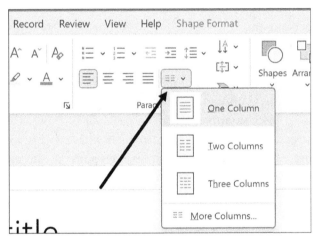

Click on the dropdown arrow and then click on the number of columns you want. If you click on the More Columns option at the bottom, that will open the Columns dialogue box where you can choose any number of columns you want as well as set the spacing between the columns.

Here is an example of the three columns option when I only have enough text for a column and a half:

> This is text that I'm adding to this presentation so that we have enough text to see how multiple columns work in a text box.
>
> Let's go ahead and add yet another paragraph here so that we have plenty of text to work with.
>
> And maybe one more.
>
> Okay, good enough.

It's not very pretty, but it is a good example of how this works. PowerPoint took the text box (the black outline you can see) and divided it up into three sections. It then put text in the first section until that section filled, at which point it started to put text into the second section. Since I didn't have enough text to fill that second section, the bottom of the second section and the third section remain empty.

PowerPoint does not have column breaks like Word, so you can't insert a break to force text into the next column. (At least as of now, their Help specifically states this and says to submit a request if you'd like to see that.) So the only way to balance out your text across columns right now is to use Enter to add enough lines to force your text into place. Not ideal.

The nice thing about using columns is that your text will flow between the columns. But, if your text is pretty static and you want more control over what text appears where, it's probably just as easy to insert three identical text boxes and paste your text into each separate box.

So if you need multiple columns I'd experiment and see which approach works the best for you.

Line Spacing

Another way you can format lines of text is by changing the spacing either between the lines within a paragraph or between different paragraphs of text. For this one, I usually just right-click and choose Paragraph to use the Paragraph dialogue box.

Here are two paragraphs of text. For the first one the spacing between the lines of text within the paragraph is set to .9 which is the default. For the second one it is set to 1.9 which you can see in the dialogue box:

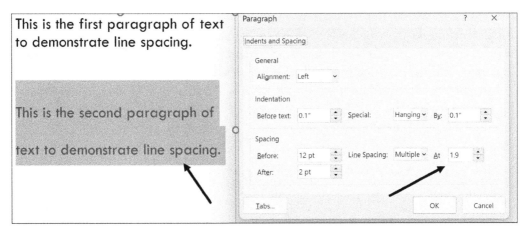

There is a significant difference there, right? That second set of lines don't even look like they belong together they're so far apart.

That Line Spacing dropdown has choices available for single, 1.5, double, exactly, and multiple line spacing. For exactly and multiple line spacing you can then add a value.

Now let's look at the spacing between two paragraphs. I've changed both paragraphs back to .9 spacing between the lines within the paragraph, but now I want to adjust the space between them.

To do that I either need to adjust the After value for the first paragraph or the Before value for the second paragraph.

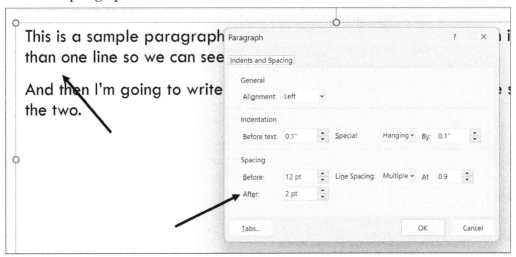

Here I've changed the Before value for the second paragraph to 12. You can see that there's about a line's worth of space between the two paragraphs when I do that.

If two paragraphs have different settings, so maybe one says 2 pt after and the other says 12 pt before and those overlap, PowerPoint combines the two values. So you get a 14 pt space.

Which means that sometimes if you're trying to fix spacing between two paragraphs you will have to look at the settings for both of them to figure out where that value is.

As I mentioned at the start of this section, I tend to right-click and choose Paragraph and go from there. But the mini formatting menu has a line spacing option that can appear on the right-hand side that lets you choose between 1.0, 1.5, 2.0, 2.5, and 3.0 line spacing.

The Line Spacing option is also in the top row of the Paragraph section of the Home tab:

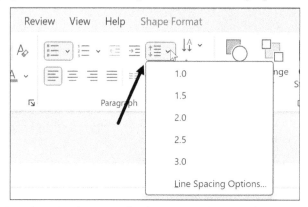

If you click on Line Spacing Options at the bottom of either list it will open the Paragraph dialogue box.

Special Types of Indentation

One final item to discuss in that Paragraph dialogue box. In the Indentation section there is an option for Special with a dropdown menu that lets you choose between none, First Line, and Hanging and then lets you specify a value.

First line will take the first line of a paragraph and indent the text from the left side by a set amount but keep the rest of the lines in that paragraph aligned normally. You can see an example of that in almost all of the paragraphs in most print books. The first paragraph of a section or chapter usually doesn't do this, but every other paragraph usually does.

So if you need that for a paragraph, open the Paragraph dialogue box, choose First Line, and then set the value for indent.

Hanging does the exact opposite. It leaves the first line alone but then indents the rest of the lines of text. This is often used with a bulleted or numbered list where text wraps to the next line so that the text in each line of the paragraph starts at the same point. If you don't set the text to have a hanging indent then the second line of the paragraph will align with the bullet point or number instead.

* * *

Alright, so that's formatting text and paragraphs. A lot of basic beginner presentations just use text so that's where we're going to stop in this book. Because we still need to talk about how to give your presentation and all the fun little bits that go with that. If you want to use tables or charts or SmartArt or any of that, it's covered in the next book in this series.

Animations

If you've ever given a presentation, then you know the annoying feeling when you're trying to talk and your audience is scanning ahead on the current presentation slide rather than listening to you. That's where animations come in handy in PowerPoint. You can design the presentation so that each line of text or element on the slide appears separately.

Animation is added after the slide has been prepared, so enter all the text you want on that slide and then click onto the first line of text and go to the Animations tab:

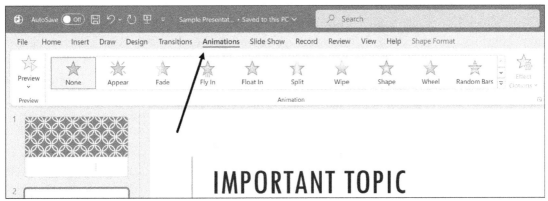

You can see here that there are a large number of animation options. You can have text appear, fade, fly in, float in, split, wipe, shape, etc., etc.

You do you, but I will tell you this from the perspective of someone who has given presentations to thousands of people at a time and also had to sit through hundreds of business presentations, that often the simplest approach (appear) is the best.

Remember, your presentation is there to support what you're trying to say, not to steal the show.

Just my opinion, but maybe ask yourself if this contributes to what you were trying to do or not when you're tempted to go a little overboard in terms of special effects.

Okay, lecture done.

Click on the type of animation you want to use from that Animation section of the Animations tab. PowerPoint will then add that type of animation to *all* of the bullet points in that slide that are at that level:

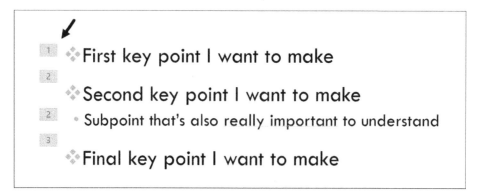

It will also number the items to show you the order in which they will appear.

So if you look at the image above, you can see that my first bullet point is numbered one but then the next two are numbered two. They're going to both appear at the same time unless I change that, because one is a subpoint so initially grouped with the main point. Finally, we have the third main bullet point which will appear third.

Most times I don't want the sub-point to appear at the same time as my main point. So I don't want the second and third line above to appear together. Which means I need to fix that. How do I do that?

First step is to click on the expansion arrow in the bottom of the Animation section of the Animations tab:

This will bring up the Appear dialogue box. Click over to the Text Animation tab:

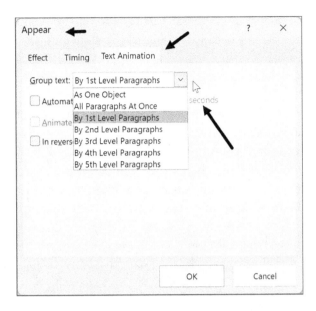

From there you can change the Group Text dropdown option. The default is By 1st Level Paragraphs which is why my subpoint is not set to appear separately.

In my presentation slide I only have two levels of points, so I could choose By 2nd Level Paragraphs and it would work just fine. But if I had a more complex slide then maybe I'd need to use By 5th Level Paragraphs to get each sub-subpoint to appear separately.

I made my choice and now you can see that each line of text will appear separately:

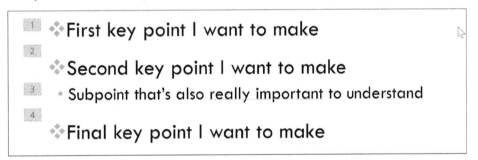

Perfect.

But I still want to see what I've set up. (Often this is crucial when there are photos or videos or other non-text elements on the slide.)

For me, the best way to test a slide like this is to just go to the Slide Show tab and start a presentation from that slide. (We'll cover that momentarily.)

Bring that up and then either left-click, use the down arrow, use the right arrow, or hit Enter when you want the next line to appear. Each of those options will show the next item or advance you to the next slide if there's nothing left. Esc to exit that preview.

There is also a Preview option on the left-hand side of the Animations tab, but it won't work with default settings. That's because it "plays" the slide and the default setting for these animations is to have no delay set up. Which is absolutely fine when you're up there clicking through and giving your presentation. But when you're trying to "play" the presentation, everything hits at once.

If you want to use that option, you need to go to the Timing section of the Animations tab and change the Delay value to something like 00:50. That will give enough of a delay for you to see each element appear by itself.

Keep in mind, too, that if you use the Appear animation it will just have the line show up on the slide. If you really want to see animations at work try one like Fly In or Float In. As you click on each new option the slide should "run" and show you that effect without you needing to Preview.

Another preview option is to click on Animation Pane in the top row of the Advanced Animation section. That will bring up the Animation Pane task pane that will also let you "play" your presentation.

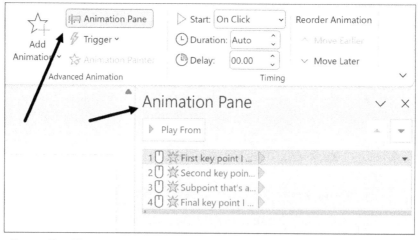

Setting up bullet points like I did above is relatively easy to do. But sometimes I have different elements on my slides or I want the main points visible right away but not the subpoints. The way to create a more complex order is to use this Animation Pane.

As you can see above, it shows each of the animated items for that slide and the order in which they will appear. Each line also has symbols that are supposed to tell you what will make that line appear (a click by default which is represented by that white image of a computer mouse) and what type of animation will be used. Next to that you can see the text that starts that specific line.

It's better though to hold your cursor over each item to see a text description of what will happen. Because when I was just now experimenting with different animation styles on the same slide that little green star didn't change all that much:

And yet each of those first three lines there uses a different animation. You can see in the image above that I've held my mouse over that third line and it uses the Split animation style.

To do what I was just doing and apply different types of animation to different lines of text in your presentation (something that's probably not a good idea due to the distraction factor), just select each line individually and then click on the animation you want.

Okay, back to the Animation Pane.

When you click on a specific item in the Animation Pane, there's a dropdown arrow that appears at the very end of that line. Left-click on that arrow to choose a different way to start the line. Your options are click, with previous item, or after previous item by a set period of time.

Usually click is the option you want. But if you're going to have the slide run on its own for an audience, then the after previous item option would let that happen. Finally, with previous item will group two of your elements together so they appear at the same time.

For example, let's say you have two subpoints and you want both of those to appear together, but you don't want the third subpoint to appear just yet. You can't use the level setting we discussed before because it would apply the same rule to all three. But what you can do is go to the second of the two subpoints (assuming it's already set to appear after the first subpoint), and change the timing option for that second subpoint to Start With Previous. That should make both of those items appear at the same time.

To change the order in which an item appears, click on that line in the Animation Pane, and then use the up and down arrows at the top of the pane to move the item around in the numbered list. That will change the item number on the slide as well:

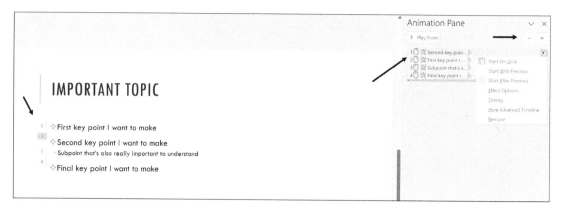

Here I moved that first line to the second appearance position and it is now numbered 2. If I run this slide, you will see "Second key point…" appear before "First key point…"

In the image above, the horizontal black arrow on the right-hand side is pointing to the up and down arrows you can use to shift an item up or down in the order.

You can also see the dropdown menu for that first row, which has the start options as well as timing and effect options. Those are also available in the Advanced Animation and Timing sections of the Animations tab.

If you expand your list of animation choices in the Animation section of the Animations tab, you'll see that there are also animation options for placing emphasis on an item in your presentation or for having an item exit your presentation. They work the exact same way.

As I said before, using animation is very handy sometimes. Just don't overdo.

Other Tips and Tricks

Before we move on to how to actually give a presentation, I wanted to touch on a few other tips or tricks that might be helpful.

Add Notes to a Slide

When I advised you to keep the text on your slides to the bare minimum, I can imagine that some of you thought to yourselves, "But then how do I remember that detail? Or what if I forget what the bullet point is about?"

Well, good news is that you can add notes to your presentation that are either, (a) visible when you print the presentation for yourself, or (b) visible on your computer as you present but not on the screen that participants see.

To add notes to your presentation slide, go to the right-hand side of the gray bar below your main workspace and click on Notes:

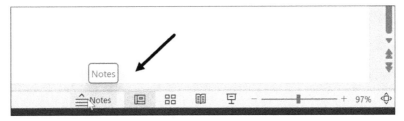

That will open a task bar at the very bottom of the screen that says "Click To Add Notes".

You can also go to the Show section of the View tab and click on the Notes option there to get the same task bar. However you manage to open it, simply click on that space and type in whatever note you want to add like I did here:

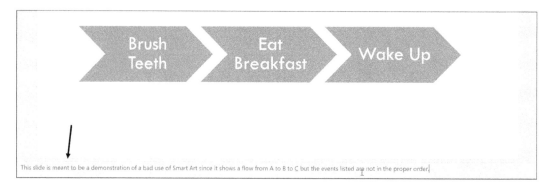

If you have a lot of text to add in the Notes section, you can make that section bigger by holding your mouse/cursor over the border between that notes pane and your slide until you see a white arrow pointing up and down. Left-click and drag upward. That will increase the size of the Notes section while decreasing the size of the slide.

We'll talk about printing later, but if you want to see how those notes look on a Notes Page printout, you can go to the Presentation Views section of the View tab and click on Notes Page. You'll see something like this:

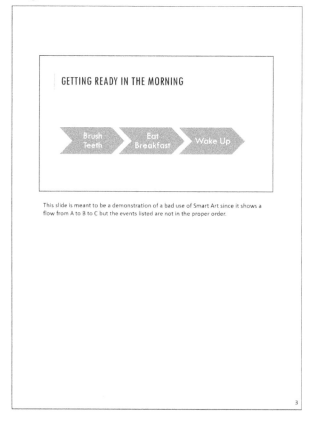

It has the slide at the top and then any added notes in the section below that. You can, if you want, print this for your participants, but remember that they will just read the notes instead of listen to you. So notes pages are best used for the presenter alone or as handouts after the fact.

To return to the standard view click on Normal in that Presentation Views section of the View tab.

Spellcheck

To run spellcheck on your presentation, go to the Proofing Section of the Review tab and click on Spelling. It should be the first option.

It works pretty much the same as in Word.

If there are no spelling errors, PowerPoint will just tell you that.

If there are spelling errors, PowerPoint will open a Spelling task pane on the right-hand side of the screen. That pane will identify the misspelled word at the top. Below that you can choose to Ignore Once, Ignore All, or Add (to the dictionary) if it's not a misspelling. If it is a misspelling, there will be a list of suggested words it could have been where you can click on one of the choices and then tell PowerPoint to Change this one instance or Change All to change all misspellings in the entire document.

If you're not sure which spelling is correct, below the suggestions box will be a definition for the currently selected option. (This can come in handy when trying to figure out whether you wanted discrete or discreet, for example.)

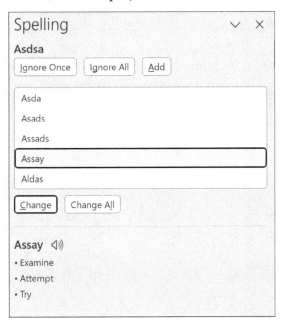

Do be careful with using Change All and Ignore All because they apply to all instances of that word and you don't get to evaluate each instance separately.

Also, just a reminder that spellcheck is not a substitute for a final readthrough. I will sometimes end up with a cuss word that I didn't mean to include because it's one letter off of the word I did mean to use. Spellcheck doesn't catch that.

It also doesn't work with similar words. Just now as I was proofing this document I had used "lest" instead of "lets". Spellcheck misses things like that. So you should read through one last time no matter what.

Find and Replace

Ctrl + F is the easiest way to find a word in your document. Using that will bring up the Find dialogue box where you can type the word you want. There are checkboxes below the field where you type what you're looking for where you can choose to match case and/or find whole words only.

So if I want to find all uses of "Tom", I'd check both of those boxes so I don't end up finding words like tomorrow as well.

Note that it does seem to also look in placeholder text that was used in a presentation. So, for example, I just searched for "to" in a presentation where I only had three slides and it brought up some slide masters that used phrases like "Click Icon To Add Picture."

If that ever happens to you and you need to get back to your presentation, go to the Slide Master tab and click on the Close Master View option.

Ctrl + H will bring up the Replace dialogue box which has fields for both what to find and what to replace it with. You also have options there for match case and find whole words only. Use them.

It can be especially important with replace to use those boxes because you don't want to accidentally turn "tomorrow" into "Steveorrow" when what you really meant to do was replace "Tom" with "Steve".

You can bring up both the Find and Replace options via the Editing section of the Home tab as well if you ever forget the control shortcuts.

Replace Font

The Editing section of the Home tab is the only place I know of where you can replace a font. Click on the dropdown arrow for Replace and you'll see an option there for Replace Fonts.

This will open the Replace Font dialogue box, which has a dropdown for which font you want to replace and which font you want to use instead. Make your choice and then click on Replace.

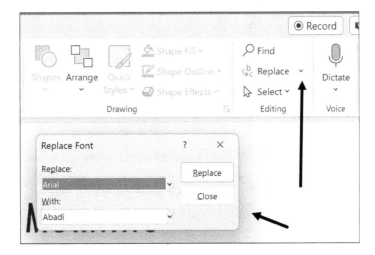

The dialogue box *does not* default to your current font so you need to know what fonts you're already using before you try this.

Also, it did not work on SmartArt for me just now, so you'll need to scan through your presentation and see if there was any text you thought should've changed but didn't.

And, finally, be careful with this if you have a lot of fancy formatting or lots of text in your presentation already, because sometimes fonts that are the same point size take up different amounts of space on the page. That means formatting that worked for your original font may not work for the replacement font and you'll need to fix that.

One more thing, it may not be perfect. I used this on a work presentation template someone had set up using a font that wasn't available. And it did replace that font in everything I can see on the slides, including the master slides. But, every single time I open that presentation it also tells me that the font I replaced is missing. So clearly somewhere it didn't get replaced, but I wasn't able to find it and neither was this replace font option.

Undo/Redo

We discussed this in the basic terminology section, but I wanted to circle back to the Undo option and also discuss Redo.

Undo will back out of what you just did. If I apply a font to text and don't like it, the easiest way to change that back is Ctrl + Z.

If you ever undo something and then change your mind and want it back, the easiest way to do that is Ctrl + Y.

But sometimes you may take multiple steps before you realize you want to undo something. For example, maybe I add a table to a presentation and I do a lot of fiddly little formatting to it where I change column widths, add text, and change colors and then at the end of the day I realize that, no, I just need to back out those last five or six steps.

In that case, the best option is the Undo arrow at the very top of the workspace. It's the arrow pointing to the left and will always be available as long as you've done something in the presentation. (If you've yet to do anything it will be grayed out.)

Click on the dropdown arrow on the right side of that Undo option, and you'll see a listing of the last X number of steps you took. Here we have sixteen steps that can be undone but the list can be longer than that:

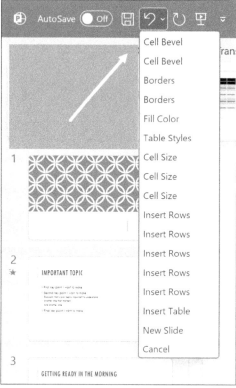

The top item is the last thing you did. The bottom item is the oldest step that you can undo.

Each item listed gives you some idea what it was about but not a great idea, so you kind of have to know what you just did or how far back you want to go.

In this case, if we look from the bottom up, I inserted a new slide, added a table, expanded that table from two rows to seven, and then started changing the column widths and messing around with formatting of the table.

If I want in one step to go back to that original inserted table without all that additional formatting, then I could click on the last of the listed "Insert Rows" entries in that list.

That undoes everything that happened after that point. I am now back to a new slide with a two-row table in it.

Now, maybe I messed that up. I undid all of that and now I have a table with only two rows and all of the columns are all the same width. But I actually wanted those five rows I'd added.

To Redo part of what I just undid, I can use Ctrl + Y or click on the arrow at the top that points to the right. Sadly, as I write this, I can only do so one step at a time. But it is pretty easy to use Ctrl + Y multiple times and I honestly rarely need to redo something I undid.

Zoom

You can zoom in or out on your presentation slides by using the slider in the bottom right corner of your workspace.

The bar perpendicular to the line shows where you currently are in terms of zoom level. The actual percentage is listed at the far right of the bar.

By default mine is zoomed to 97% for a new presentation, but that changes as additional task panes appear. When the Designer tab opens, it drops to 80%, for example.

To change the zoom level on your slide, either click on the bar to the left or right of the current marked spot or left-click on that marker and drag until the main workspace is the size you need.

You can also go to the Zoom section of the View tab and click on Zoom to bring up the Zoom dialogue box, which lets you choose from 400%, 200%, 100%, 66%, 50%, and 30%. You can also change the Zoom to Fit value to any percentage you want.

I often use this to get back to 100% when needed.

Note that with Zoom, the size of the slide changes but not the size of the workspace where the slide displays. So if you go for a high zoom percentage you will not see the full slide.

This is different from how the slide workspace will resize when you change the size of a taskpane that surrounds that workspace. So sometimes it may work better to click and drag along the edge of one of the visible task panes to make more space for the main slide area in your workspace.

Headers and Footers

If you want to print your presentation slides, chances are you may want to include headers or footers. To do so, go to the Insert tab and click on the Header & Footer option in the Text section. That will open the Header and Footer dialogue box:

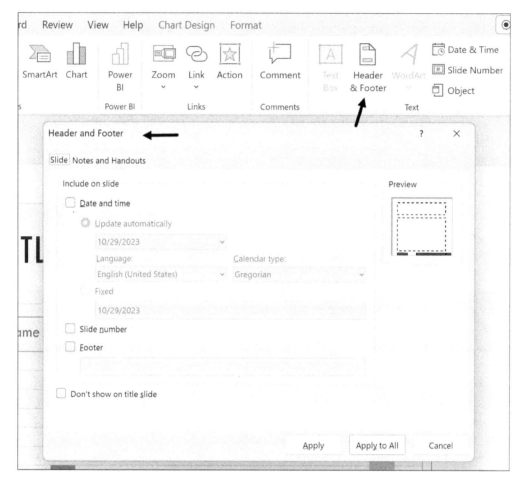

Your options for what to insert are limited. On a slide you can insert Date and Time, Slide Number, or a custom Footer.

You can also choose to not include that information on the title slide but just include it on every other slide in the presentation.

For Notes and Handouts, you can choose between Date and Time, Page Number, a Header, and a Footer.

As you click on each choice, the little thumbnail image on the right-hand side will put a black box where that element will appear. You can't change the location that element will appear in unless you go and change your master slides, which we are not going to do. So you're stuck with wherever that element is set up to appear for your chosen presentation theme.

Present Your Slides

Okay. You've created a presentation. Congrats. Now it's time to present it. How do you do that?

Go to the Start Slide Show section of the Slide Show tab, and click on From Beginning or From Current Slide on the left-hand side:

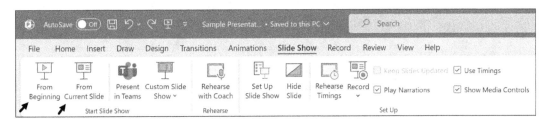

Usually you want to do From Beginning unless you're testing a presentation slide, in which case the option that lets you just start at the current slide is very handy.

If you're on a laptop or desktop computer and not connected to another monitor or anything like that, your entire screen should now be the presentation. You'll either start with the first slide or the last one you'd had selected, depending on the choice you made.

To navigate to your next slide or bring up any text on your current slide that was set to appear, you can left-click, use Enter, or try the right or down arrows.

If you ever go a little too far and want to go back a slide or a bullet point, use the up or left arrows.

You can also right-click and choose Next or Previous, but I never use that.

To exit your presentation before you're done, use Esc. Otherwise when you reach the end of the presentation the screen will be black and you'll see a message that says "End of Slide Show, Click to Exit." You can left-click or Esc will work there too.

There are some fancier options to choose from if you right-click on a presentation, like what your pointer looks like under Pointer Options, but if you're going to use them get those set up before you start presenting.

You can also see the Presenter View by right-clicking. So if you want to know what that view will look like while just working with your own screen, that's how to do that.

The Presenter View looks like this:

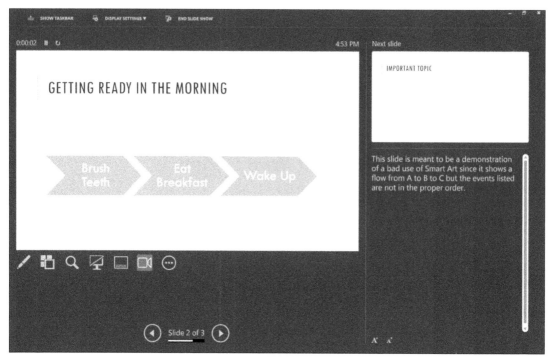

Your current slide is on the left-hand side. The notes related to that slide are on the right-hand side bottom section. Above the notes on the right-hand side, you can see which slide is up next and what it will look like when it appears.

So, for example, that next slide actually has four bullet points on it but in this preview we don't see them because when that slide comes up it will not show those automatically since I have them set to appear one at a time.

If you have your computer connected to an external monitor or a projector, Presenter View should launch automatically. The current slide will show on the external monitor or projector and your screen will show the next slide and notes.

There are some additional options below the current slide that you may want to play around with as well, but we won't cover here.

You can turn Presenter View off by right-clicking and choosing Hide Presenter View.

Print

Often it's a good idea in smaller group settings to also print your presentation slides so people can take notes as they listen to you.

You can find your print options by going to the File tab and then clicking on Print. Or use Ctrl + P. Both will bring up the Print screen:

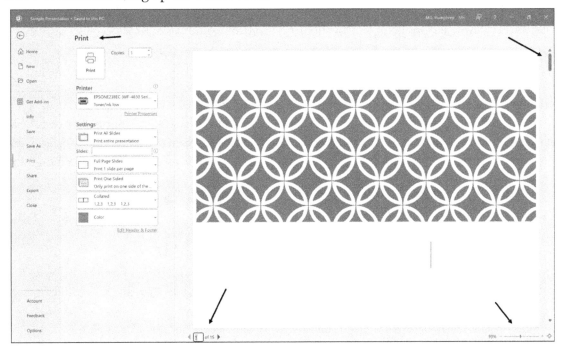

On the left-hand side in the second panel under the heading Print are your print options.

To the right of that is the preview section that takes up most of the space on the screen. That section will show you how the presentation will look when printed.

Below the preview are navigation arrows that let you move from page 1 to 2 to 3, etc. or back. There are also scrollbars on the right-hand side of the current visible slide that will let you see the other pages that are going to print. And in the bottom right corner is a slide where you can adjust the zoom level.

Now let's talk about all those settings under Print.

* * *

Print

At the very top of the print options is the button you click on to actually print. It's currently a square with a black and white icon of a printer that says Print below the icon.

Copies

Next to that is where you specify the number of copies to print. Click into the box and type the number you want or use the up and down arrows to change the value.

If you have never printed this presentation before, it might be a good idea to start with one copy and review it before you print twenty or a hundred or however many copies.

Printer

Directly below those options is a dropdown where you can select which printer to use.

Mine defaults to Microsoft Print to PDF because a few years back I noticed that if I had an Office program open and that program listed my personal printer as the default printer that it sometimes took a very long time for the program to open. So I always have to change this setting to my actual printer when I need to print.

I think the default setting is for Office to list your most recently used printer.

Printer Properties

Under the printer dropdown is a link for Printer Properties which will open a dialogue box with choices. You need to have your printer selected before you use this since the options available will be impacted by the printer you're using.

This is generally where you'd go to choose your paper or print tray if needed.

Settings

Under Settings you have a few choices to make. Make sure your printer is selected before you use this section.

Print All Slides / Print Selection / Print Current Slide / Custom Range

The first choice is which slides to print. The default is Print All Slides. That will print all of your slides.

Print Selection requires that you already selected a subset of slides before you clicked on print. Print Current Slide will print the slide that was showing in the workspace when you chose to print.

Custom Range will take you to the Slides field directly below that dropdown. You can then enter which slide numbers to include. Commas between numbers means to print each one you list. So, 3,6,9 will print slides 3, 6, and 9. But a dash between numbers means to print the range. So, 3-9 will print slides 3, 4, 5, 6, 7, 8, and 9. You can combine commas and dashes so something like 3,4,5-7 will print slides 3, 4, 5, 6, and 7.

Click away from that box and the preview section will update to show the slides that will print.

If you have sections in your document, which we did not learn in this book, the section names will also be options for you to choose at the bottom of the dropdown menu. PowerPoint will print all of the slides in that one section if you choose one of the options listed there.

Slides

If you're trying to print a custom range, you can just skip using the dropdown altogether and go straight to the Slides field and put in the slides you want. PowerPoint will change the dropdown to Custom Range for you.

Print Layout and Handouts Dropdown

The next dropdown menu defaults to Full Page Slides so that's the title you'll see, but there are a lot more options under that if you click on the dropdown arrow.

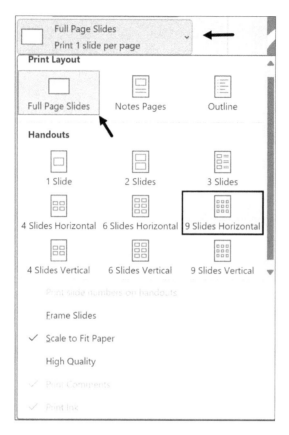

With Full Page Slides each printed page will have one slide per page and it will fill the page.

The Notes Pages option will print with your slide on the top third of the page and any notes displayed under that. So this is a good one for you as the presenter, but maybe not for your audience because you want them to listen to you not read the slides.

The Outline option just prints the freestanding text on each of the slides in a long list. It will not print the contents of tables or any images or anything else.

The 1 Slide Handout option puts the slide in the middle third of the page with open space above and below it.

The other slide handout options with 2 to 9 slides per page do exactly what they say. They fit 2, 3, 4, 6, or 9 slides onto the page arranged either vertically or horizontally. You can see what each option will look like in the preview section.

Below all those choices there are also some options that you can check or uncheck by clicking on them.

They are: Print Slide Number On Handouts, Frame Slides, Scale to Fit Paper, High Quality, Print Comments, and Print Ink. Experiment with selecting or unselecting each one until you get the preview appearance that you want.

For example, my sample presentation had comments still in it. When I went to print, PowerPoint wanted to print an entire page for one of my slides that was just the comments for that slide. It also wanted to mark that slide as having a comment on it. I didn't want that, so I had to click on the Print Comments option to uncheck it.

Print One Sided /Print on Both Sides (Long) / Print on Both Sides (Short)

The next option lets you choose whether to print on one side of the page or on both sides of the page. This will only be visible if the printer you have connected to allows that. For slides or other landscape layouts (where the top is longer than the sides) you generally want to print on both sides and flip on the short edge. For notes pages or other layouts that are longer along the side than across the top you generally will want to flip on the long edge.

Collated / Uncollated

Here you choose whether to print one presentation at a time (collated) or each page of the presentation X number of times before printing the next page (uncollated). Which choice you want will depend on whether you want people to have the full presentation up-front or whether you intend to hand out each page of the presentation as you reach it.

Color / Grayscale / Pure Black and White

This option lets you choose whether to print in color, grayscale, or pure black and white. The black and white option strips out colored sections and makes them white not black, so it's the option that will use the least amount of ink. The grayscale option keeps those colored sections but transforms them to shades of gray. It's easy enough to see what each one will look like by making your choice in the dropdown menu and then looking in the preview section.

Edit Header & Footer

At the very bottom there is a link you can click on to edit the header and footer sections of your presentation. Click on that to bring up the Header and Footer dialogue box which we discussed earlier. Note that it has two tabs, one for Slides and one for Notes and Handouts, so you need to make your choices on the correct tab.

Page numbers are always good to have. I often like to also include the name of the presentation and author even if that's already on the title slide since slides can become separated.

Conclusion

Alright, that's pretty much it for a beginner-level introduction to PowerPoint. It's probably not everything you're going to need because we didn't cover inserting tables or images into your presentations. Nor did we cover SmartArt or WordArt. But I like to keep these books to a certain length that isn't too overwhelming and I think we've hit that point. So I'll cover the rest of that in the next book in the series.

If you don't want to continue on with me, you can, now that you have the basics, use PowerPoint's help options to get the rest of the way there.

In PowerPoint 365 as it exists in October 2023, Help can be found as a separate tab on the far right set of the tab choices. Click there and you'll see five options: Help, Contact Support, Feedback, Show Training, and What's New.

For users of 365, it's probably especially important to occasionally check in on that What's New option because 365 is constantly evolving, and sometimes the changes may be big ones or ones that would make your life easier if you knew about them. They certainly have been with Excel over the last couple years where some really great new functions have been added.

If you click on the What's New option it should open a task pane on the right-hand side of the workspace that has links to what they've added recently.

(Of course, nothing is ever perfect so when I was writing the first draft of this book that wasn't working for me at the time. The problem with all these connected options is that sometimes that connection fails and then you have nothing there.)

Anyway.

Help works the same way. You click on the Help option in the Help section of the Help tab and it opens a Help task pane where you can look up a topic that you want to learn more about:

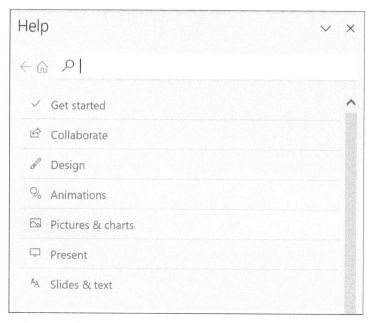

Either use the search bar at the top or click on one of the topics listed there to see more about that topic. There's text descriptions as well as videos.

You can also usually just hold your mouse or cursor over each of the options under a tab and PowerPoint will give you a description for that particular task. Like here where I held my mouse over the Shapes option:

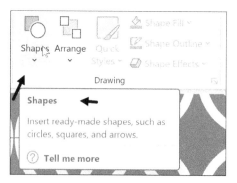

Often those descriptions have a Tell Me More choice that you can click on to bring up Help specific to that option. That will once again open the Help task pane, but this time to that particular topic.

Now, what do you do when Office has put all of their help topics online and your version of PowerPoint seems to not be willing to connect to them like, oh, I don't know, me when I was writing the first draft of this section?

You can always do an internet search. I usually type "microsoft powerpoint 365" and then whatever topic I'm trying to learn about like "shapes".

Often the top result or one of the top results is from the Microsoft website. I look for links that say support.microsoft.com first or in this case the top link was microsoft.com. Those are the best place to start. Microsoft has really good help available, it's usually going to be up-to-date, and you don't risk clicking on something you shouldn't.

Google these days also has little answers to questions they pull onto their search results. Sometimes those work, too. They also tend to offer video links, which often are also good resources.

Personally, I tend to avoid watching random Office videos online because I once found a great helpful video on a topic that answered my question wonderfully only to realize that it was a complete rip-off of a video someone else had done a year before that.

Since I try not to reward assholes for being assholes that copy the hard work of others, that made me avoid random dude on the internet publishing tech help videos. But you do you. If you need the answer, you need the answer. I just always try to start with the official resource first.

Okay, so that's about it. Reach out if you have a question and can't find the answer. I don't check email every day these days, but I do check in and will try to help. And if you want to learn more from me then check out the next book in this series, *Intermediate PowerPoint 365* which covers tables, images, videos, SmartArt, and more.

Index

Delete Slide 48

Designer Task Pane 23–24, 35–37, 51–52, 54

Dialogue Box

Definition 13

Dropdown Menu

Definition 12

Duplicate Slide 47–48

E

Esc 87, 99, 111

Expansion Arrow

Definition 13

F

Find 106

Footers 109–110, 117

Format Painter 86–87

Format Text

Bold 68–69

Change Case 70–71

Clear Formatting 77

Color 71–73

Columns 91–92

Direction 75–76

Font 69–70

Indent 59, 85–86, 94

Italicize 74

Line Spacing 92–94

Paragraphs 79

Size 73–74

Text Alignment 87–91

Underline 76–77

H

Headers 109–110, 117

Help 119–121

M

Master Slides 60

Microsoft 365 1, 119

Mini Formatting Menu 68–69

Definition 16

Move File 28

About the Author

M.L. Humphrey is a former stockbroker with a degree in Economics from Stanford and an MBA from Wharton who has spent close to twenty years as a regulator and consultant in the financial services industry.

You can reach M.L. at mlhumphreywriter@gmail.com or at mlhumphrey.com.

www.ingramcontent.com/pod-product-compliance
Lightning Source LLC
LaVergne TN
LVHW081346050326
832903LV00024B/1339